Things You Don't Know About Heaven

JUDSON CORNWALL

Charisma
HOUSE
A STRANG COMPANY

Most STRANG COMMUNICATIONS/CHARISMA HOUSE/SILOAM/
FRONTLINE/REALMS products are available at special quantity
discounts for bulk purchase for sales promotions, premiums,
fund-raising, and educational needs. For details, write Strang
Communications/Charisma House/Siloam/FrontLine/Realms,
600 Rinehart Road, Lake Mary, Florida 32746, or telephone
(407) 333-0600.

THINGS YOU DON'T KNOW ABOUT HEAVEN
by Judson Cornwall
Published by Charisma House
A Strang Company
600 Rinehart Road
Lake Mary, Florida 32746
www.charismahouse.com

Unless otherwise noted, all Scripture quotations are from the King
James Version of the Bible.

Scripture quotations marked AMP are from the Amplified Bible.
Old Testament copyright © 1965, 1987 by the Zondervan Corpora-
tion. The Amplified New Testament copyright © 1954, 1958, 1987
by the Lockman Foundation. Used by permission.

Scripture quotations marked JB are from the Jerusalem Bible, copyright © 1966, 1967, 1968 by Darton, Longman and Todd Ltd and
Doubleday, a division of Random House, Inc.

Scripture quotations marked NEB are from the New English Bible
(New Testament), copyright © 1961 by Oxford and Cambridge
University Press.

Scripture quotations marked NKJV are from the New King James
Version of the Bible. Copyright © 1979, 1980, 1982 by Thomas
Nelson, Inc., publishers. Used by permission.

Portions of this book were previously published as *Heaven*, copyright © 1978, by Bible Voice, Inc., ISBN 0-89728-008-3.

Cover Designer: studiogearbox.com
Design Director: Bill Johnson

Library of Congress Cataloging-in-Publication Data
Cornwall, Judson.
   Things you don't know about heaven / Judson Cornwall. -- 1st ed.
     p. cm.
  Rev. ed. of: Heaven.
  Includes bibliographical references (p.   ) and index.
  ISBN 978-1-59979-096-1 (trade paper)
  1. Heaven--Christianity. I. Cornwall, Judson. Heaven. II. Title.

BT846.3.C67 2007
236'.24--dc22

2007002138

07 08 09 10 11 — 9 8 7 6 5 4 3
Printed in the United States of America

To my father, E. James Cornwall (1901–1973), a devoted minister of the gospel, a teacher of God's Word;

and

To my wife's father, Donald G. Eaton (1900–1969), a faithful Christian layman, a tiller of the soil.

ACKNOWLEDGMENTS

S INCE THIS BOOK was not my idea, I want to thank George Otis, formerly of Bible Voice, for encouraging me to write the original version and for trusting me with his dream.

I would like to express my deep appreciation to my wife, Eleanor Cornwall, for the many hours of companionship she sacrificed in order that I might push the completion of this book. She sat silently in many motel rooms while I wrote and pulled a pillow over her head to drown out the noise of my typewriter in the early morning hours and late at night after the conference service had ended. She read the early drafts and offered criticism, checked the Scripture references of the final draft, and encouraged me to continue when I got discouraged with the work.

When I consider thy heavens, the work of thy fingers, the moon and the stars, which thou hast ordained; what is man, that thou art mindful of him? and the son of man, that thou visitest him?

—PSALM 8:3–4

CONTENTS

Preface: About This Book. xi

Introduction: Embarking for Heaven. xv

1 Is Heaven a Real Place?. 1

2 What Is Heaven Like? 13

3 How Different Will Our Heavenly Home Be
From Our Earthly Home? 31

4 Where Is It, and How Do We Get There?. 43

5 The New Jerusalem: Fact or Fiction?. 59

6 What Will the New Jerusalem Be Like? 69

7 How Different Will the New Earth Be
From the Old Earth? 89

8 What Will Life in Heaven Be Like?. 109

9 Will We Rule on the New Earth?. 125

10 What Will My Body Look Like?. 135

11 Will I Recognize Loved Ones? 147

Epilogue: Prayer—the Link Between
Time and Eternity 155

Notes 159

Scripture Index 165

About This Book

FOLLOWING THE EVENTS of 9/11, many people returned to their spiritual roots in search of truth about life after death. In the weeks after, churches and synagogues experienced record numbers in attendance. During those times of uncertainty in our nation, probably foremost on the minds of most Americans were questions like: *Is there really a heaven and a hell? If heaven really does exist, how do I get there? Will I ever see my loved ones who have passed away?* These are some of the questions answered in this book.

Sociologists from Baylor University's Institute for Studies of Religion wrote and analyzed a seventy-seven-question survey conducted by Gallup on 1,721 Americans on their view of God. About 92 percent said they believed in God, a higher power, or a cosmic force.[1] Within this group emerged four different perceptions of who God is and how He relates to mankind. They were authoritarian, benevolent, critical, or distant. Of the four categories, the Authoritarian God, which is viewed as a God who is angry at humanity's sins and engaged in every creature's life and world affairs, was the most recognized. Of those surveyed, 31.4 percent held this view, with 43.3 percent in the South.[2]

Among those surveyed, most people thought that their loved ones are going to heaven. Those surveyed felt that the "pearly gates open widest for family (75.3% say they'll get in) and personal friends (69.3%). The survey did not ask whether people expect to go to heaven themselves."[3]

It is unfortunate that most Americans view God as someone who is angry. What does that say about our relationship with Him? Where has the church neglected to show the world that the loving, yet righteous, God longs to spend eternity with them? If this is who God is, then why would anyone want to go to heaven to be with Him?

WHY THIS BOOK?

One of Judson Cornwall's close friends, George Otis, encouraged the beloved Bible scholar and evangelist to write a book on the subject of heaven. Some of the staff members of Bible Voice had heard a sermon series on heaven by Judson Cornwall and were convinced that he needed to publish a book on it. Although somewhat hesitant at first, Judson wrote the book *Heaven*, published by Bible Voice. That was nearly three decades ago. Since that time, there has been a paradigm shift in theology, societal viewpoints regarding the afterlife, and an increase in the material on this topic, particularly heaven and hell.

Judson Cornwall's writing will challenge you to stretch your faith and preconceived ideas of what heaven will be like. Whether you agree or disagree with Cornwall's theological viewpoints is not as relevant as the hope that you will search the Scriptures for yourself to pique your interest about where *you* will spend eternity. Even if you have professed Jesus Christ as Lord and Savior and know you will be in heaven someday, this book will offer you a fresh perspective of it.

As for Judson Cornwall, after a long battle with cancer, he went home to be with the Lord in 2005. In a final interview with *Charisma* magazine founder and publisher, Stephen Strang, Judson's response to facing his death sentence was, "I don't see death as a cessation of life, but as stepping into that heavenly realm."[4] He was concerned that the church had moved away from teaching on heaven and that it was time for the body of Christ to return to her spiritual roots: "I'm afraid that today's generation is so caught up with the here and now that we're no longer concerned with the hereafter."[5]

We need to ask ourselves: Have we have focused so much on this life that it has shifted our attention away from heaven? The Word urges to "seek those things which are above, where Christ is" (Colossians 3:1, NKJV). Jesus encouraged us to "seek first the kingdom of God and His righteousness" (Matthew 6:33, NKJV). Our focus should be on spending eternity with Him. Basilea Schlink, in his book on the realities of heaven and hell, said:

> We are to live with our lives focused on heaven. Jesus came to earth for this very purpose and God shapes our lives accordingly, so that heaven will have more and more room in our hearts. It is Jesus' deep longing that heaven draw closer to us and eternity become a reality for us, for in the same measure will He, the Lord and King of heaven, become a reality for us.[6]

Judson lived his life focused on his Lord and heaven. No doubt his family, friends, and those of us who knew Judson miss him, but he left behind a spiritual inheritance through his teaching materials and his literature that inspires us to seek a deeper relationship with God and a longing for going home.

—LILLIAN LAITMAN-MCANALLY
Developmental Editor

INTRODUCTION

Embarking for Heaven

I HAVE PRAYED EARNESTLY and have applied myself diligently to be able to share what the Scriptures clearly teach about heaven, and I have used testimonies, dreams, and visions of others only as additional color from time to time. Yet the greatest challenge is preparing to embark for heaven.

The moment of stepping from this life into the next should not be one we dread or fear. Every child of God is waiting for that moment. It will be a very quick process, a joyful process. Instantly we are caught up into the presence of God. Jesus said that He would be there to gather us; He will meet us. This life on Earth is nothing more than a short-term time of preparation for our eternal life in heaven. Heaven is God's home, His abode, and He is going to share that home with me—with you. His presence with us will be the joy of heaven.

I want to help you to know what I have learned about preparing to embark on my trip to heaven. No, I don't want to tell you what possessions to purchase for the trip, what luggage to pack, or what airline to travel on.

Preparing to make that final trip to heaven does not involve any of the trappings of this life on Earth. Your preparation for heaven is more important than any preparations you may have completed for a trip in this earthly realm in

THINGS YOU DON'T KNOW ABOUT HEAVEN

which you live. We must be prepared to enter a different realm—a spiritual realm where we will live forever with our Lord.

During my lifetime of service to my Lord, I have been doing my best to prepare for heaven. But that preparation rose to an entirely new level when I received my death sentence from the lips of my doctor. Many months passed after that moment. How long has it been since your death sentence was served? Have you, like me, realized that you had precious few moments left to make your final preparations for the time when you will step from this life into eternity? Are you prepared to embark for heaven?

"I haven't been served a death sentence yet," you may say. You are wrong. Perhaps physically you are not facing death. However, the Bible teaches us that when Adam, the first representative of mankind, sinned in the Garden of Eden, his sin brought death to the entire human race. Not only did natural death to our physical bodies enter the scene, but spiritual death, involving eternal separation from God, also became a sad reality for all of mankind. My death sentence issued by the doctor is not as devastating as the death sentence over every life that has not acknowledged this biblical reality of eternal damnation, referred to in Scripture as the "second death" (Revelation 20:12–14).

ANTICIPATING HEAVEN

Those who have died in Christ have not been cheated out of life; they have been metamorphosed into the real life. And the best part about that real life will be seeing Jesus face-to-face. John tells us, "We shall see him as he is" (1 John 3:2).

Heaven would be glorious even without this, but after seeing Him as He really is—not as we have imagined Him to be—heaven's joys will be absolutely overwhelming. Moses is the only man in the Bible who was afforded the privilege of face-to-face communication with God, but in heaven it will be available to all of us. If just knowing Him through the letters He wrote (the Bible) has made Christ so precious, try to picture what it will do to us when we actually behold Him intimately.

The beauties of heaven and unhindered life with God Himself defy our imagination. I have read the testimonies of several who have had near-death experiences that took them into heaven, and each was significantly different from the others.

The Scriptures do give us a few glimpses beyond the veil. John, the beloved disciple, gives us quite a graphic picture of heaven in the Book of Revelation. He presents it as a beautiful city with walls of jasper and streets of gold. Much of this revelation is what I will share with you in this book.

To understand spiritual mysteries requires a point of reference for them to even be describable. We have no such point of reference available to us, for heaven is so unlike Earth as to defy even our wildest imaginations. But we can still try!

Close your eyes, and mentally visualize the most beautiful scene you can. Fill it with flowers, animals, people, or whatever is heavenly to you. Surround yourself with angels, and mentally visualize the presence of God. Perhaps you imagine the most beautiful music you have ever heard, while seeing colors so vivid that they seem to almost speak to you. Sniff the aroma that only heaven could produce, and then multiply this ecstasy by a million times, and you would still be far from an accurate description of the heaven God has prepared for His children.

SOMEDAY . . . IN HEAVEN

What great grace it will be to live forever with Jesus. But that is a grace He has given to me in this life. Incredible as it seems, I enjoy His loving presence before I die. I am especially conscious of the nearness of His presence now that I have been made aware of how near my exodus is.

I am discovering that His grace is both sufficient and available when it is needed. I will lack nothing I need to make the death transition into endless life with God. The timing and the method are all in God's hands, and He does all things well.

If this book can make the reader even half as homesick for heaven as it has made the author, it will have been worth all of the labor.

You and I will meet, someday, in heaven.

CHAPTER 1

Is Heaven a Real Place?

S IMPLY ANSWERED, YES. One main point emphasized throughout this book is that heaven is a real place, prepared for real people.

It is not without significance that an inner awareness of a real heaven has been placed so strongly in the heart of man. There is not a single religion on the face of the earth that does not make a provision for a heaven. The view and concept of that heaven varies greatly, but some sort of utopia beyond this life must be offered to satisfy the inner craving that exists.

God the Creator programmed into man strong desires for what would be available to him and good for him. The newborn baby, who has always been automatically fed from the bloodstream of the mother, calls for food shortly after birth although it cannot intellectually understand the concept of food and its availability. All of man's basic instincts function before, and sometimes in spite of, his understanding.

Among these many drives, or instincts, that God has built into the human being is a belief in and a yearning for heaven. These very yearnings argue favorably for the existence of a literal, real heaven that will satisfy these God-given cravings, for in satisfying every other propensity with which we were born, we have found substance and reality;

1

surely there is an actuality to meet this craving as well. God would never cause us to desire a heaven if there were no heaven to satisfy that desire. I have heard preachers excitedly proclaim, "God has given us a little bit of heaven on Earth." I believe that. We now have a taste for and even a foretaste of heaven, but what is yet to come will satisfy our every need and longing.

Most people believe in hell, but does anyone still believe in heaven? Hell is real enough in our concept to be used as a comparative term or as the basis for an oath. Without this concept of hell, those who swear would be very limited in their vocabularies.

Sadly, what is true of the common concepts of most communities is equally true of the celestial concepts of most churches. Most of religion believes and preaches hell but shies away from presenting a literal heaven.

Not only has the church been guilty of speaking more of eternal punishment than eternal rewards, but it has also shied away from the concept of a literal heaven and substituted "spiritual concepts" in its place. How often is the whole subject of heaven dismissed with, "Where Jesus is, 'tis heaven there." Of course! But where is Jesus? Certainly He must have a bigger dwelling place than "in my heart," for that would make me heaven and my heart the throne of God.

There was a day when the church believed, preached, and looked for a literal heaven where man could share God's home forever. Perhaps the encroachment of secularism and worldly culture distorted this picture, and perhaps the church merely ceased to try to give substance to that which Western civilization had secularized. During the nineteenth century the concept of heaven became increasingly vague, and the twentieth century prostituted what vestige of heaven remained. The word *heaven* was used usually in connection with dreams, love, lyrics, and fiction, until it has been divested of any true concept. In the twenty-first century, the pendulum is beginning to swing in the opposite direction. As our world becomes increasingly volatile and we are robbed of the security and self-sufficiency we once leaned upon, humanity is searching for a place where safety, peace, and security are not compromised.

But just because the world has plagiarized, polluted, and profaned the word *heaven*, that does not take away from its reality; it merely distracts our attention from it. No amount of labeling lust as "heaven on Earth" can destroy the eternal place God has prepared for His redeemed ones. One of Satan's favorite tricks, when he has been unsuccessful in destroying faith, is to make the terminology of the Scriptures so secular and common that it loses its sense of reality. But "we are not ignorant of his devices" (2 Corinthians 2:11). While the world may mean one thing when it says "heaven," the Christian should certainly mean something far different.

Another one of Satan's tricks is to lie and convince us that he is not real. There's a quote that says, "The greatest trick the devil ever played was convincing the world he didn't exist." If he can deceive us into thinking he isn't real, then he can deceive us into thinking hell (or heaven) is not real. It is part of his nature to lie: "When he speaks a falsehood, he speaks what is natural to him, for he is a liar [himself] and the father of lies and of all that is false" (John 8:44, AMP). The enemy slanders God's name and His dwelling place (Revelation 13:6)—heaven—as if any attempt to discredit God and His home would do away with both.

SEVEN COMMON MYTHS DEBUNKED

Why is it that every time one of our brothers or sisters gets close to crossing from this life to the next, we form special prayer chains to try to talk God out of taking our friend to heaven? Perhaps it is because our perception of what heaven will be like is skewed by misconceptions. Over the years of preaching the gospel as a pastor and a teacher, I have found seven popular misconceptions of heaven firmly fixed in the minds of most people, especially Christians.

1. "Heaven is what you make of your life now."

One of these is the simple statement that heaven or hell is what you make of life right here on Earth. This asserts that you make your own heaven; you make your own hell. A Hollywood actor once stated that he didn't necessarily believe that heaven and hell occur in another life. He thought they were happening now. What a tragic display of ego to think that any of us is big enough to create our own heaven or hell; heaven is not created by man, but for man. It is not the apex of his present existence; it is the residence for his eternal existence. Man does not *earn* heaven; he *enters* it.

2. "This life is an extension of heaven."

A second misconception some have about heaven is that it is merely an extension of this life; it is only located somewhere else. In their understanding, nothing changes but the location. If this is true, who needs a heaven? Let's simply regain access to the tree of life and live forever right here.

Heaven is an actual place.

3. "At least when I die, I'll finally get to rest."

The third misconception is that heaven is a place of inactivity. Many people—including some Christians—believe that its inhabitants will sit on fleecy clouds, strum harps, and sing hymns. It will not be a time of "eternal rest," a perpetual vacation. Man was made for activity, not inactivity. Perpetual leisure has always been destructive to men.

Heaven will be a place of rest *and* activity. In heaven we will:

- Enjoy eating and drinking (Isaiah 25:6; Luke 14:15; 22:30; Revelation 2:7)

- Enjoy the beauty of God's creation—flowers, trees, and so on (Ezekiel 47:7, 12; Revelation 22:2)

- Observe animals (Isaiah 65:25)

- Build houses and plant crops (Isaiah 65:21)

- Sing, play music, and worship before God's throne (Isaiah 51:11; 66:22–23; Revelation 14:2–3)

Heaven will be a place where we can rest from our labors as well as rest in God's provision. We will be rid of our fears, anxieties, pains, strife, and griefs. There will be no tears there.

4. "Heaven will be one long praise and worship service."

A fourth misunderstanding is that heaven is a place of perpetual praise and worship—one continuous watch night service for billions times billions of eons. I admit that heaven is filled with praise, but as I noted above, it is also filled with activity in addition to this worship. There is probably no greater delight than to know that not only will we sing to God, but we will also listen as He sings over us (Zephaniah 3:17). That will be the most beautiful sound of all!

5. "We will experience all the pleasures of Earth with none of the negativity."

Another misconception about heaven is that it is a place of sensual pleasure. People who believe this see heaven as a place where inexhaustible sensual appetites are being gratified continuously and to their ultimate. This is a commonly held belief among Muslims. According to the Quran, those who go to heaven will have virgins and experience sexual pleasures (Surah 56:35–38). But we know that we will not have sex in heaven. How do we know that? We will not marry or be given in marriage (Matthew 22:29–30). God ordained marriage and sex within marriage so that we would procreate (Genesis 1:28; Psalm 128:3) and so that we would enjoy relational intimacy between a husband and a wife. Thus, in heaven, we will experience the deepest levels of intimacy in our relationship with Christ.

6. "When I get to heaven, I'll know everything."

A sixth misinterpretation of heaven that I have heard Christians express is that heaven is a place of complete knowledge, as if all the wisdom of the ages is going to be imparted to them by osmosis: "When I get there, everything I ever wanted to know will be made known to me. I'll merely absorb it from the presence of God." If this is so, then why does God put such a premium on our learning while still here in this life? (See Proverbs 2; 3; 18:15.) In Revelation 6:10, the martyrs ask God a question, and in the next verse He answers them. This proves that some things we won't know; otherwise, why would these martyrs ask God a question if they knew everything?

7. "In heaven, our bodies will be ghostly figures."

There are others who believe the term "glorified bodies" signifies that we will have translucent bodies and will travel around like disembodied spirits. If that were true, then why did Jesus appear as flesh and blood after His resurrection? (See Luke 24.) In heaven we will have incorruptible bodies that will not be subjected to death and decay (1 Corinthians 15:52–54).

If these views, and others that are equally weak and unscriptural, are so common among today's Christians, then we can better understand why there is so little excitement about going to heaven.

We will expose some of these myths in later chapters.

MANY NAMES, ONE PLACE

To help us further in our conception of God having a specific place that He considers "home," the Bible uses at least six different words that refer to heaven, and all of them contain the idea of a dwelling or habitation.

The fundamental word is *tabernacle*, which refers both to the tabernacle built by Israel in the wilderness and the "true tabernacle, which the Lord pitched, and not man" (Hebrews 8:2). In the preface to my book on the tabernacle, I point out that "the Old Testament devotes fifty chapters to describing the tabernacle (in the wilderness) and the Book of Hebrews devotes forty-three percent of its content (131 out of 303 verses) to giving us its spiritual meaning. The Holy Spirit is repeatedly trying to teach us principles of heaven."[1]

The Book of Hebrews tells us that the tabernacle with all of its ritual and sacrifices was a "shadow of heavenly things," and Moses was repeatedly commanded to "make all things according to the pattern shewed to thee in the mount" (Hebrews 8:5). The three courts of this tabernacle speak, in part, of the three levels of the heavens, starting from God's abode and reaching out to man's court, the outer court. The closer the priest came into the presence of God, the more elaborate, ornate, and costly the surroundings were, and the simpler the worship was.

The stated purpose of the tabernacle was that God might dwell with His people and that those people could have access to His presence. Jesus became that tabernacle, enabling God to come among men in a recognizable way, and gave these men a more direct access to God than they had ever known: "The Word was made flesh, and dwelt among us [Greek *skénoó*, which means "to tent or encamp"; specifically, to reside]" (John 1:14).

But beyond bringing an access to the presence of God unto men, the tabernacle in the wilderness and the Tabernacle not made with hands (Christ Jesus) both give us a visual picture of God inhabiting a dwelling place. The fact that Moses was shown something and then told to reproduce it in a portable form, and that the Book of Hebrews tells us this was but a shadow of God's heaven, confirms and reinforces the declaration of the Scriptures that there is a real, literal heaven. God has an abiding place to which we have been invited. It is called heaven, and it is pictured in the tabernacle.

In spite of the many Bible chapters devoted to the story of the tabernacle, the word that appears with the greatest frequency in reference to heaven is the word *house*. Jacob referred to Bethel, where he had his great vision, as "the house of God" (Genesis 28:17), and Solomon called the beautiful temple he built a "house" (1 Kings 8:27). Even Jesus referred to heaven as "my Father's house" (John 14:2). This expression is one with which we can all readily identify, for we regularly associate house and residence. Few of us think of "house" without equating it with "home." In speaking of heaven as a house, we strip it of all of the unseeable majesty and glory and visualize it as something with which we can be comfortable.

Closely related to these two concepts is the word *temple*, which is also substituted for heaven in the Scriptures. A good example of this substitution is in David's song commemorating God's delivering him out of the hand of Saul. He sang, "In my distress I called upon the LORD, and cried to my God: and he did hear my voice out of his temple" (2 Samuel 22:7). But an even more familiar example is in Isaiah's vision of God: "I saw also the Lord sitting upon a throne, high and lifted up, and his train filled the temple" (Isaiah 6:1). Perhaps the word *temple* gives a greater sense of permanence than tabernacle does, but both speak of a dwelling place for God and a meeting place between God and men.

The innermost court of both the tabernacle and the temple was sometimes referred to as the *sanctuary*, and this word is occasionally used as a euphemism for heaven. The writer of the Book of Hebrews uses this word in speaking of Christ our high priest as being "a minister of the sanctuary" (Hebrews 8:2), and the psalmist obviously refers to heaven when he writes, "For he hath looked down from the height of his sanctuary; from heaven did the LORD behold the earth" (Psalm 102:19). In so speaking, the writers were equating the holiest part of the dwelling place of God on the earth with

His eternal habitation—heaven.

Similarly, in both the Old and New Testaments, heaven is often called the *throne* of God (Isaiah 66:1; Matthew 5:34; and others). As we will see later, the Book of Revelation is greatly involved with this throne of God, which seems to be the center of heaven's government. We are even told to bring our needs to "the throne of grace" (Hebrews 4:16), which is only another way of saying to pray to God in heaven.

The word *glory* is sometimes used as an expression of heaven. While Stephen was being stoned, he "looked up stedfastly into heaven, and saw the glory of God, and Jesus standing on the right hand of God" (Acts 7:55), and in describing the ascension of Christ, Paul wrote that He was "received up into glory" (1 Timothy 3:16). Even our hope of entering heaven is termed "the hope of glory" (Colossians 1:27). Since throughout Scripture the glory of God is a physical, visible, manifestation of the presence of God, it becomes natural to equate this with the heaven of God.

These six words that are sometimes used in place of "heaven" in the Scriptures bring an even stronger sense of the reality of a literal heaven, for each refers to something very real, tangible, and demonstrable. To these writers heaven was as real as the tabernacle or the temple. They visualized heaven as the Father's house, or as His sanctuary, or throne. They were saying that heaven had substance…heaven was real…heaven was an actual place, just as these things were. Although the Bible describes much of the spiritual qualities of heaven and the availability of many of its benefits to believers right here and now, there is nothing in any of its sixty-six books that would take away from the consistent teaching that heaven is a real place, prepared for real people, who will enjoy its benefits in real bodies.

Moreover, the Bible declares that heaven exists now, not sometime in the distant future. It is God's eternal home at this time. It is the present residence of the angels of God, who are mentioned at least 170 times in the New Testament alone. It is the resting place and sphere of activity of those victorious saints who have preceded us in death (Hebrews 12:22) and is the command post, so to speak, of all of God's activities throughout His wide realm of creation.

In spite of this limited physical evidence of a literal heaven, many of today's Christians insist on spiritualizing heaven. No wonder so many professed believers are anxious to put off getting into heaven as long as the doctor's skill can keep them out! It has been many years since I have heard a Christian testify to homesickness for heaven, and even longer since I have heard a sermon extolling the joys of heaven. Perhaps it is because this generation has a heaven without substance. Their heaven has no reality; there is nothing that the soul can reach out and grab. To them heaven is an ambiguous, nebulous nothing that is reputed to follow the death of the believer—and they are supposed to really enjoy it if they ever get there.

This world's vision of heaven is little more than a void of shadows, of mists, and of dim visions of blessedness—but without reality. Tragically, many Christians' visions of heaven lack as much substance as the world's concept. They have spiritualized all of God's teachings about heaven and have brought them into the here-and-now until they have nothing left for the hereafter. They have no city, for they say that is the corporeal church on Earth. They have no throne; they equate that to their hearts. They have no dwelling places, no gardens, no animals, and no food supplies for the future; they somehow make figures out of the facts and then apply these things to something in the present time, leaving them no substance for the future.

But God has marvelously "given unto us exceeding great and precious promises: that by these ye might be partakers of the divine nature, having escaped the corruption that is in the world through lust" (2 Peter 1:4). Therefore, it makes it unnecessary for us to make a type out of an antitype, or to chase shadows while turning our backs on the substance. If we will remember that the Hebrew word for *heaven* is neither singular nor plural, but dual, we can realize that there are glorious spiritual aspects of heaven available to us here and now without violating the clear statements of the Scriptures about a concrete, solid, real, substantive heaven.

CHAPTER 2

What Is Heaven Like?

WHENEVER I MINISTERED to people in third world countries who have had very limited contact with the world beyond their communities, some have asked me, "What is America like?" I was always at a loss for an answer.

If a foreigner asked you to describe America, how would you answer them? If you have spent most of your life in New York City, you would very likely describe America as a huge, bustling metropolis, the center of trade, commerce, and culture. If you have lived your life in the great Wheat Belt of our central plains, you would describe America accordingly. The westerner would speak of the beautiful mountains and the blue Pacific Ocean, while the resident of the northern states would more likely speak of innumerable lakes and flowing rivers. Could the governor of Alaska agree with the description of America that a Hawaiian native might give? The politician and the poet would paint vastly different word portraits of this great country, and the educator and the evangelist might have very divergent views about America.

Who is right? Everyone! America is too vast, too complex, and too varied to be described from any single point of view. We would need not only various geographic descriptions but also the viewpoints of our many nationalities that have merged to form one nation. We would need to project some understanding of our economic strength as well as our political structure. It takes many ingredients to form a balanced picture of America. Similarly, it will take more than one perspective to get a balanced concept of what heaven is truly like.

Since the material universe preceded sin and will outdate sin, I find it necessary to take a very literal view of heaven. I expect it to be a material heaven. I expect it to be as prepared for whatever nature of body I will have then as this earth was prepared for the form of body God made for Adam. Heaven is as real as Earth is real, and it is prepared for people who are spirit, soul, and body as surely as the earth was prepared for people who are spirit, soul, and body. However, this does not mean that heaven is only a continuation of the earth or of mortal life without sin.

In the New Testament, heaven is spoken of as paradise, as the Father's house, as the New Jerusalem, and as Zion. They are one and the same place, but various provisions and diverse functions are described. Paradise is heaven's garden; the Father's house is heaven's housing; the New Jerusalem is heaven's city; and Zion is heaven's governmental monarchy. The concepts are not competitive; they are completive. Until we have seen them all, we will not understand the whole.

In suggesting that the New Testament gives us four different characterizations of heaven, I do not suggest that there are four separate heavens—merely that no one description could adequately depict the place that God has prepared for them that love Him. In this chapter we will take a closer look at the significance of heaven. Let us begin by examining the biblical description of it.

HOW DOES THE BIBLE DESCRIBE HEAVEN?

Years ago I preached an extended series of sermons on heaven—much of that material has become the basis for this book. A few months after the series ended, my youngest daughter, Tina, had a very serious automobile accident and lay unconscious for several days. When she finally regained her senses in the intensive care unit of the hospital, she whispered to me, "Oh, Daddy, it's just like you described it, only far more beautiful. I felt like I had been there before, because of your preaching, but it was so wonderful I didn't want to leave it. If Jesus Himself hadn't come to me and told me that my time on Earth was not up, I would have stayed forever."

Since then I have talked with several people who have had extensive visions of this paradise of God, and the more they told me about it, the more homesick I became for heaven. They have told me that while much of it looks like the most beautiful portions of this earth, even more looks like nothing we have ever seen in this world. They were impressed with the complete perfection they saw everywhere and the absolute absence of withered leaves or dying vegetation. There was no sign of aging, no incident of infirmity, no unpleasantness, and no unwholesome desires.

Briefly, let's look at seven things that God's Book tells us about heaven.

1. Heaven is beauty beyond explanation.

First, it teaches us that heaven is going to be light and beauty beyond anything man can comprehend: "Eye hath not seen, nor ear heard, neither have entered into the heart of man, the things which God hath prepared for them that love him" (1 Corinthians 2:9). Just as the mole boring in the depths of the earth, living its entire life from birth through death beneath the surface of this planet, cannot comprehend or visualize the beauty on the surface, so we who were born beneath heaven are equally incapable of imagining what heaven is like. Even if one returned to Earth from heaven and tried to describe it, we would be unable to grasp what he was saying, for there would be nothing in our realm of experience to which we could liken it.

2. In heaven we will receive a higher level of understanding.

Second, we understand that heaven will be a place of great enlargement of knowledge. In his beautiful eulogy on faith, Paul declared, "For now we see through a glass, darkly; but then face to face: now I know in part; but then shall I know even as also I am known" (1 Corinthians 13:12). Heaven will offer many answers to Earth's puzzles.

Theological mysteries that once perplexed us will be revealed. God will make the hidden things known:

> He reveals deep and hidden things; he knows what
> lies in darkness, and light dwells with him.
> —DANIEL 2:22, NIV

3. Heaven is a place of service.

Also, heaven is going to be a place of service. Revelation 7:15 says, "Therefore are they before the throne of God, and serve him day and night in his temple." When God placed man and woman in the Garden of Eden (the original paradise), He gave the man instructions to "tend and care for it" (Genesis 2:15, TLB).

There will be time for praising and worshiping God, but there will be time for service, too, because service is another form of worship.

4. Heaven is a place of endless joy.

According to Revelation 21:4, heaven is a place of joy. This is consistent with Christ's impartation of joy to His disciples and His assurance that He desired both His joy to remain in them and for their joy to be full (John 15:11).

5. Heaven is a place of safety and security.

I understand that heaven is going to be a place of stability or permanence: no more moves, no fear of being "bumped" or replaced. One of the reasons we hesitate in responding to some of the beautiful positives of life is that we are so afraid that they will be taken away from us. There is no permanence here. But when we get to heaven, everything will be perpetual, and we can enjoy it to the fullest because we know that no one is going to snatch it away from us.

6. Heaven is a place of fellowship with others.

According to Hebrews 12:22–23, heaven is going to be a place of social joys. These verses say that we will come into the presence of several distinct groups of individuals, including God the Father, the angels, the church of the first-born, the saints who have preceded us, and others. We will not be sent off into a corner to sit out eternity with no pain. We were created to be sociable creatures. Sometimes relationships can be complicated. But in heaven, interpersonal complications, misunderstandings, and the like will cease to exist as we enter into a harmonious relationship with others. We are going to enjoy being with other believers and in God's presence, which leads me to the final point on what heaven is like.

7. Heaven is where we will fellowship with Christ forever.

Fellowship with God is why we were created in the first place. The Word tells us that heaven is going to be a place of fellowship with Christ:

> Wherein ye greatly rejoice, though now for a season, if need be, ye are in heaviness through manifold temptations: That the trial of your faith, being much more precious than of gold that perisheth, though it be tried with fire, might be found unto praise and honour and glory at the appearing of Jesus Christ: Whom having not seen, ye love; in whom, though now ye see him not, yet believing, ye rejoice with joy unspeakable and full of glory: Receiving the end of your faith, even the salvation of your souls.
>
> —1 PETER 1:6–9

Though we presently endure the hardships of this life, we press on because of our love for Him and the hope that we will be reunited with Christ forever.

Now, admittedly, these are very broad comprehensions, but they are very real. But we need to have more intricate, specific, and detailed concepts of heaven if it is ever to become as real in our consciousness as it was in the mind of Christ Jesus.

DOES PARADISE TRULY EXIST, OR IS IT ANOTHER WORD FOR HEAVEN?

Both the Old and the New Testaments speak of paradise. In the Old Testament the Hebrew word for *paradise* is translated as "an orchard" (Song of Solomon 4:13; Ecclesiastes 2:5) and "a forest" (Nehemiah 2:8), probably because it is actually a Persian word, *pairidaeza*, that was coined to describe the magnificent parks and gardens that were designed for the Persian kings. Later, the Latin scholars who produced the Septuagint version of the Old Testament Scriptures (a translation from Hebrew into Greek) used this word as a name for the Garden of Eden. Whereas our English Bible calls the first habitation of God's special creation "Eden," the Greek translation calls Adam's home "paradise."

Since Greek is the original language of the New Testament, it is quite normal that this word *paradise* would be used freely. When Jesus spoke forgiveness to the thief on the cross, He said, "To day shalt thou be with me in *paradise*" (Luke 23:43, emphasis added). Here Jesus obviously named His Father's abode as "paradise," placing this word for "heaven." Similarly, when Paul wrote about being caught up into heaven, he declared that "he was caught up into *paradise...*" (2 Corinthians 12:4, emphasis added), and yet in verse 2 he had spoken of his experience as being "caught up to the third heaven." The same placing of "paradise" for "heaven" occurs in Christ's promise to the church in Ephesus, when He told them, "To him that overcometh will I give to eat of the tree of life, which is in the midst of the paradise of God" (Revelation 2:7).

In addition to these three occurrences is the story that Jesus told of the rich man and the beggar Lazarus. (See Luke 16:19–31.) Jesus related that the angels carried Lazarus to "Abraham's bosom," which some Bible commentators express as a substitute for paradise. This substitution was frequently done by the rabbis of the day to whom Abraham's bosom and paradise were interchangeable words; the one spoke more of the place, and the other spoke more of the personalities involved in that place. If this is true, then Jesus taught that the righteous dead are carried to paradise, awaiting the fulfillment of time until the resurrection of the righteous from the dead. But whether the word used was "Abraham's bosom" or "paradise," it is always placed in strong contrast to Hades, the place of torment for the unrighteous dead who are awaiting their judgment and subsequent sentence to be cast into the lake of fire, which burns forever.

So "paradise," first seen in Eden, was uttered on the lips of a dying Savior, was visited by Paul, and became part of the introduction of the book of the consummation of all things—the Book of Revelation. But wherever we meet it, it has one common denominator: it is a place that God has prepared for His people who are awaiting the return of the Lord Jesus Christ after their earthly life has expired.

Paradise's initial description is in the book of beginnings, Genesis, where we are told about the beauties, comforts, and perpetual supply of the Garden of Eden—paradise. But in spite of all the luxurious comforts the garden offered, the two most outstanding features were the tree of life and the presence of God. By regularly eating the fruit from the tree of life, Adam entered into eternal life. So powerful was the effect of this tree that even though Adam was thrust out of paradise because of his sin, he lived to be nine hundred thirty years of age, and probably not more than one hundred of these years were spent in paradise. (See Genesis 5:3, 5.) While Adam lived in paradise, the Lord came to him in the cool of the day to walk and talk with him. What intimate communion; what fellowship! How Adam must have missed it during the last eight hundred or so years of his life.

Do we go to heaven (or hell) immediately, or does the soul sleep?

When Jesus spoke of paradise, He reemphasized the availability of these two paramount features: the tree of life and fellowship with God. In the story about Lazarus, the beggar, Jesus made it clear that this righteous man did not go into Hades to be tormented, nor did he go into a place of soul-sleep. He said that "the beggar died, and was carried by the angels into Abraham's bosom" (Luke 16:22). Immediately upon death, the soul returns to the Creator (Ecclesiastes 12:7). When posed with a question about any distinction between life that occurs at the Rapture and life immediately following death, Smith Wigglesworth replied:

> No. Those asleep in Jesus have the same life, but they are not asleep in the grave. They fall asleep to rest, but it is not a sleep or a rest of the spirit. The spirit never sleeps; the soul never sleeps.... The moment the body is put to rest, the spirit requires no rest; it is always young, it will know nothing about time.
>
> Whichever way the body goes, it will be the same. If it goes to the grave, what will happen? The body, all that is earthly, will pass away; it will come to dust. Suppose it goes up. The Word of God says it will be dissolved. The same thing, it will be dissolved either way it goes. Why? Because flesh and blood are not going there, but the life of the Son of God is. God will provide a new body, resembling the old in every way—likeness, character, everything. The human spirit will enter into a celestial body whether it goes up or down.[1]

While our mortal bodies rest until Resurrection Day, our soul is cognizant of heaven's existence. (See Daniel 12:2; 2 Corinthians 5:8.)

God has prepared a place that is a place of life, not a place of death, for prepared people. In the meantime, they wait for the Lord to "descend from heaven with a shout, with the voice of the archangel, and with the trump of God: and the dead in Christ shall rise first: Then we which are alive and remain shall be caught up together with them in the clouds, to meet the Lord in the air: and so shall we ever be with the Lord" (1 Thessalonians 4:16–17).

While the story emphasizes that the rich man "was buried," it contrasts this by telling us that the angels carried Lazarus to Abraham's side. How comforting it is to know that the angels never take us to the grave; they take us to paradise. Some people talk incessantly about "the death angel," but the Bible speaks of the life angel. It is an angel of life that has been commissioned to watch over those of us who are to become "heirs of salvation" (Hebrews 1:14). None of us need an angel to cause us to die; the sin that is warring in our members will eventually produce death. But there is a living angel who has been commissioned by God to pick us up the very moment our heart stops beating and our lungs cease breathing and to carry us directly to paradise.

Paradise means animation, not annihilation. The limited glimpse given us in this story shows us that there is memory, communication, feeling, conscience, and recognition in paradise. The loss of a functioning body does not mean the loss of dynamic life for the Christian.

By tracing paradise back to Eden we may think that paradise had its beginnings on the earth, but that is not true. In telling the story of the construction of Eden, the Genesis account speaks of "every plant of the field *before* it was in the earth, and every herb of the field *before* it grew," and then it tells us that "the LORD God *planted* a garden…in Eden" (Genesis 2:5, 8, emphasis added). Hebrew scholars have told us that the word we have translated as "planted" literally means "transplanted." God had all the plants and herbs before He formed the garden; He merely transplanted a portion of heaven's paradise into man's world in order to share the beauties of His home with man. Adam lived in a miniature heaven: his private paradise. But sin made him unfit for such holy habitation, and he was driven out while the entrance to the garden was sealed off forever.

WHERE IS PARADISE?

In the days of Christ, paradise was thought of as being within the earth and was, as we have seen, called Abraham's bosom. At the resurrection of Christ there was a mass transfer of these inhabitants from the depths of the earth to the heights of heaven. Paul assures us that "when he [Christ] ascended up on high, he led captivity captive" (Ephesians 4:8; quoted from Psalm 68:18). When Christ came forth from the grave, He not only walked out victorious over death, but He also led the inhabitants of paradise out of separation from God's presence right into the heavens. As proof of this, Matthew records that "the graves were opened; and many bodies of the saints which slept arose, and came out of the graves after his resurrection, and went into the holy city, and appeared unto many" (Matthew 27:52–53). Death could not keep its prey, and paradise would no longer be a compartment of Sheol (if it ever was). Jesus Christ moved all of paradise back into the heavenlies with Himself. His ascension was shared by these Old Testament saints who had been packed and ready for "moving day" from the moment Christ had preached to them after His death.

This completed the cycle. The paradise planted on the earth, and then limitedly made available under the earth, has been returned to the heavens where it originated. Now, for the believer, when we say "good night" here, we say "good morning" up there. Paul said, "Now we look forward with confidence to our heavenly bodies, realizing that every moment we spend in these earthly bodies is time spent away from our eternal home in heaven with Jesus.... And we are not afraid, but are quite content to die, for then we will be at home with the Lord" (2 Corinthians 5:6, 8, TLB). Since paradise has been returned to the presence of God, the Christian dead are not merely called "the righteous dead," but "the dead in Christ" (1 Thessalonians 4:16). The medical examiner may have pronounced them "dead," but God has pronounced them "in Christ."

God has a memorial park in heaven that is waiting for the "spirits of just men made perfect" (Hebrews 12:23), but it is not a memorial to the dead; it is a memorial to the living. It is not sold in plots five-by-ten feet, nor do they put people in it; they lead them to it. No one brings them flowers; they pick their own from the living plants in the garden. The gold-paved streets are not for the mourners or the funeral processions; they are for the comfort and convenience of the residents of this magnificent park. Paradise is a living place for living people.

These citizens of paradise have access to something that has been denied men since the fall of Adam: the tree of life. There will be no more dying there, nor will there be sickness, pain, or suffering, for the curse of sin will have been forever removed from these people.

But paradise is not only a place of life on a higher plane; it is also a place where fellowship with God has been restored. Jesus gave assurance to the thief on the cross that on the very day of his death he would join Jesus in paradise. No waiting, no purging period, no soul sleep until all the saints are ready to be taken to heaven; the very day that he would die with Christ was to be the day that he would live with Him.

Just as the overcomer is promised access to the tree of life (Revelation 2:7), so he is also promised, "To him that overcometh will I grant to sit with me in my throne, even as I also overcame, and am set down with my Father in his throne" (Revelation 3:21). The victorious believer is given access not only to life but also to God. Just as Adam fellowshiped with God, the heavenly residents enjoy a personal association with Him, for all that Adam lost for mankind through his sin, Jesus has restored to them through His sacrificial death. Life and fellowship with God were the chief characteristics of Adam's paradise, and they are now the prime qualities of God's paradise. When it was man's paradise, it was defilable, but from Jesus's days on Earth to the final words in Revelation it has been renamed "paradise of God." Now nothing can ruin it, for it is under a divine protectorate; it is part of God's heaven. [1]

PARADISE IS A REAL PLACE.

Just what this paradise is like defies description. Much interest has been aroused in life after death in the past years, and those who have had glimpses of the outskirts of this beautiful home of the departed saints have been most impressed with its magnitude and beauty, its light, and its music.

Over the years individuals who have had near-death experiences that allowed them to walk through sections of this garden have written many books. In order to describe what they saw, they had to use, of course, earthly comparisons, but their descriptions surpass any earthly beauty that I have ever seen in my travels.

One man who had suffered a heart attack while on the operating table shared his out-of-body experience with me. He sensed himself rising higher and higher as though borne on wings, and he saw a glistening city in the distance. He, just as others have been, was particularly overwhelmed by the beauty of the music that came from this city. He told me it seemed as if everything in the city was contributing to the music and that everything was in complete harmony. As he approached the gate he was stopped for a moment, and Jesus stepped outside the gate and stood in front of him.

"Listen to the beautiful harmony of My heaven," Christ said to this man, "and then listen to the tremendous discord in your own spirit. Could you be content to spend an eternity where you are so completely out of tune with everything here? Return to Earth and get in tune with My world."

Then the Lord touched his chest with His finger, and the man was aware of the greatest pain he had ever experienced. He began a rapid descent to Earth and was aware of falling back into his body, which was lying on the operating table. He later learned that the pain he had felt was the doctor hastily cutting open his chest to massage his heart back into action.

Beauty, perfection, harmony, music, wholeness, glory, happiness, peace, contentment, and fulfillment are words that these people have used to try to describe the overall picture of the paradise of God, but they are insufficient.

Paul, who also walked in this garden, said that he "heard things which must not and cannot be put into human language" (2 Corinthians 12:4, JB). All since him have found this same limitation of expression after getting a fleeting glimpse of the things that God has prepared for the overcomer.

One thing that runs consistently through the teachings of Jesus and through the testimonies of those who have been allowed glimpses into paradise is the fact that paradise is a real place inhabited by real people, people who are not disembodied spirits wandering around waiting to be reunited with their bodies.

Paul, who had a glimpse into paradise, said:

> For we know that when this tent we live in now is taken down—when we die and leave these bodies—we will have wonderful new bodies in heaven, homes that will be ours forevermore, made for us by God himself, and not by human hands. How weary we grow of our present bodies. This is why we look forward eagerly to the day when we shall have heavenly bodies which we shall put on like new clothes: For we shall not be merely spirits without bodies. These earthly bodies make us groan and sigh, but we wouldn't like to think of dying and having no bodies at all. We want to slip into our new bodies so that these dying bodies will, as it were, be swallowed up by everlasting life. This is what God has prepared for us and, as a guarantee, he has given us his Holy Spirit.
>
> —2 Corinthians 5:1–5, TLB

Those who have died in Christ are forever removed from temptation and satanic pressure. They enjoy the company of the angels and fellowship with God. They enjoy seminars that are taught by Isaiah, Paul, and others. They enjoy the artistry of the greatest musicians, poets, and painters. They may be restricted to heaven's garden—they haven't come into the complete fullness of heaven—but what they have is so superior to anything we have here that it is most certainly heaven to them.

Paradise is always a definite place. It is described in Genesis 2; it is lost in Genesis 3; its restoration is foretold in Luke 23; it is seen by Paul in 2 Corinthians 12; it is promised to the overcomer in Revelation 2; and it is completely restored in Revelation 22. Surely our battles, struggles, wrestling with sin, overcoming temptation, and bringing the flesh into submission to the spirit are a small price to pay for such a prize. Paradise is for "him that overcometh." Surely it would pose no problem for God to bind Satan immediately and cast him into the depths of the bottomless pit, or into the lake of fire, and to see to it that we have no more trouble, struggle, or trial now. But if He did, we would not have anything to overcome. And it is necessary to overcome in order to "come over" to Paradise. Peter recognized this when he wrote, "Dear friends, don't be bewildered or surprised when you go through the fiery trials ahead, for this is no strange, unusual thing that is going to happen to you. Instead, be really glad—because these trials will make you partners with Christ in his suffering, and afterwards you will have the wonderful joy of sharing his glory in that coming day when it will be displayed" (1 Peter 4:12–13, TLB).

Just what is it that we must overcome? It would be anything that takes divine life away from us. Life overcomes death, and Christ has given us His life right here on the earth. There will be no struggle for possession of our spirit at the moment our body dies. We settle that while we are still very much alive in the flesh. When the angel comes to lead us to our heavenly home, Satan argues our right of entrance, for Christ's gift of life automatically makes us overcomers. We gain our citizenship rights before we ever enter paradise.

CHAPTER 3

How Different Will Our Heavenly Home Be From Our Earthly Home?

TRAVELED WIDELY IN my teaching ministry, and sometimes I would get exhausted. On those occasions, all I could think of was going home. Home is a place of rest and peace for me. It is a place of escape from the pressures of this life and a place of tranquility that allows the inner tempest to be stilled.

When we think of home, we usually think of it as the place where we are loved for our own sake...a place where we are always welcome...a place where we can retire from the strife of the world and enjoy rest and peace. Home, to the child, is a place of safety and security. It is a place of unlimited provision and a place of intimate love that binds the family unit together. Home, to the adult, is often viewed as a place of reunion, where the scattered family gathers again around the father's table for renewed fellowship. To those who have enjoyed a good home, it is a fitting symbol of heaven, and for those who were cheated out of a good home life, heaven will make it up to them.

As Jesus approached the final few weeks of His life on Earth, He repeatedly tried to prepare His disciples for the separation that was imminent. "To My Father's house," was

Jesus's simple answer. "I'm going home to prepare a place for you."

Ever since Jesus introduced the term "My Father's house," it has been a favorite concept of heaven for most Christians. *Home!* Believers are now in a strange country, in an enemy's land, and, like soldiers serving on a lonely post, we dream of going home.

But this is more than just home—*it is the Father's house,* His residence. It is even more than the Father's house; it is *"my* Father's house." After His resurrection Jesus told Mary, "Go to my brethren, and say unto them, I ascend unto my Father, and your Father; and to my God, and your God" (John 20:17).

He is our God, our Father, and it is to our Father's house that Jesus has gone to prepare a place for us. This greatly enhances our sense of security and love. Paul wrote:

> For I am convinced that nothing can ever separate us from his love. Death can't, and life can't. The angels won't, and all the powers of hell itself cannot keep God's love away. Our fears for today, our worries about tomorrow, or where we are—high above the sky, or in the deepest ocean—nothing will ever be able to separate us from the love of God demonstrated by our Lord Jesus Christ when he died for us.
>
> —ROMANS 8:38–39, TLB

If this is true now, while we are only under the protection of His hand, how much more will it be true when we are under the protection of His house?

In the last hours of fellowship Jesus bluntly stated, "Where I am going you cannot follow Me now, but you shall follow Me afterward" (John 13:36, NKJV). This completely confused the disciples, who had spent about three years following Jesus *everywhere* He went. Boastful Peter insisted that nothing would keep him from following Jesus, but he was humiliated when Jesus told him that before daybreak he would have denied any relationship to Jesus three times.

Because Jesus knew He was going to come from the grave with His resurrected body, He did not speak of going to paradise; He was going directly to the Father's house as the firstfruits of the resurrection.

Jesus was the only one who ever spoke of heaven as the Father's house, but He did so on three separate occasions. Of the temple in Jerusalem He said, "Make not my Father's house an house of merchandise" (John 2:16). Although in the Old Testament the temple had been called the "house of God," only Jesus could call it "My Father's house." He dared to refer to the earthly structure as His Father's house because it was there that the symbol of God's presence rested; it was there that He was worshiped, and it was there that His people communed with Him. It was the Father's house on Earth by design, dedication, and function. But when the religious leaders rejected Christ as God's Son, Jesus disowned the temple, saying, "Behold, *your* house is left unto you desolate" (Matthew 23:38, emphasis added). In this last scripture, Jesus indicates that the glory of the Lord had departed, and it was no longer God's house.

Unlimited Resources and Unconditional Love

Another time Jesus spoke of the Father's house was in the parable of the prodigal son. When the son returned, a great welcome-home banquet was prepared in his father's house, and the feasting was accompanied with music and dancing (Luke 15:25). The prodigal son discovered there was a fatted calf, an extra robe, a reserved ring, a choir, an orchestra, and dancers all awaiting his arrival.

And so it will be for us when we arrive in heaven: "No good thing will he withhold from them that walk uprightly" (Psalm 84:11), and "Fear not, little flock; for it is your Father's good pleasure to give you the kingdom" (Luke 12:32). Our Father's house is obviously a place of joy, festivity, unconditional love, and endless supply.

For those of us who lived through the Great Depression, we know what it feels like when the provisions of our earthly father's house run dangerously low, but there is no possibility of shortages in our heavenly Father's house. He who created the entire universe with the word of His mouth will never lack anything that His children need.

When we read of a father's house in the Old Testament, we are immediately confronted with a family, a household, a clan, a whole tribe, or even a nation. It was a term that denoted many people whose common denominator was a shared progenitor: one father, many descendants. Thus Abraham could become the "father of many nations."

When Jesus spoke of "My Father's house," He spoke not only of a definite place, but He also implied a great progeny who could trace their ancestry back to a new birth with God as the Father. The fact that Father's house has "many nations" indicates that this is a large, diverse family. On Earth, large families can sometimes spell trouble, for being fathered by the same man does not, in itself, produce tranquil relationships among the siblings. In heaven, however, there will be no arguments in our Father's house, no competition, no drive to excel over another, and no desire to belittle another. All responsibilities will be equally shared among its inhabitants, so no one will feel that he is overworked. The emotional tenor of the place will be relaxing, and so will the atmosphere of the home.

The more family members, the more love is needed to bind that family unit together. The children do not originate the love; they merely respond to it and reflect it. As has so often been said, the greatest thing a father can do for his child is to love his wife consistently. A harmonious "love flow," if you will, between husband and wife forms the basis for the security and well-being of the children, and it gives them a constant example of proper, interpersonal relationships.

One of the joys of our Father's house is the consistency of love that flows between God the Father and God the Son. In His high priestly prayer, Jesus prayed, "Father...thou lovedst me before the foundation of the world" (John 17:24). Jesus demonstrated His great love for the Father in humbling Himself and becoming obedient to the death of the cross.

The love of the Father flows out to us, His children, as well. Basilea Schlink describes it beautifully:

> We shall only be able to comprehend the ineffable glory of heaven if we have fathomed the depths of the love of God—love that since the beginning of time has had nothing but plans for showering His children with all good things. And when we enter heaven, we shall be utterly overwhelmed by this love of His.[1]

When we get to the Father's house, we will be surrounded by a love that breaks down prejudices, melts hardness of heart, blends that which is divergent into a united whole, and generally makes a family out of many children. We will no longer be brothers and sisters in name only, but we will be merged into a family whose filial responses are joyful, responsible, considerate, and consistent. When we get home to the Father's house, it will be not only a family reunion, but also a genuine uniting of that family. His love for us will become our love for one another; we will truly love with His love.

A ROOM—OR A HOME—OF ONE'S OWN?

As Jesus told His disciples that He was preceding them to "[His] Father's house," He added that there were "many mansions" (John 14:2). The Greek word we have translated "mansion" is used only twice in the New Testament, both times in this chapter. In verse 23, "Jesus answered and said unto him, If a man love me, he will keep my words: and my Father will love him, and we will come unto him, and make our *abode* with him" (emphasis added). Because the second use of this word seems to have a more spiritual application than a literal one, some preachers spiritualize away the "mansions" Jesus spoke of by translating it as "placements." Then they point out the differing levels of Christian service and relationships that are available while we are still here on Earth.

But this does not stand up to good scholarship. Jesus was speaking to bewildered, confused, despondent disciples who couldn't fully grasp that Christ was going to leave them. In answer to their question about where He was going, Jesus told them, "Let not your heart be troubled: ye believe in God, believe also in me" (John 14:1). They were concerned with a literal separation from Christ and His actual ascension into heaven. They wanted to go with Him; they feared separation from Him. To give them a basis for faith instead of fear, He told them that He was going to the Father's house, where there were many mansions, in order to prepare a place for them to come and be with Him. Would it have comforted them to be told that there were many spiritual levels here on Earth where God could place them? No! They wanted to go with Jesus, and He was going to a very real heaven that He called "Father's house."

Men who have devoted their entire lives to the study of New Testament Greek and have translated the New Testament into English always translate this verse consistent with the King James translators' use of the word "mansions." Look at some of the translations:

- "Many dwelling places"—New English Bible, The Modern Language New Testament, New American Standard, and Amplified

- "Many rooms"—Phillips, Jerusalem Bible, Revised Standard Version, New International Version, and English Standard Version

- "Many homes"—The Living Bible

- "Many dwellings"—Wycliffe New Testament

I could list a few more English translations of the New Testament, and all of them translate this word as a definite place. None of them spiritualize it as levels of appreciation of God.

Jesus taught His disciples that there are distinct dwelling places in His Father's house—durable dwellings. Our living here may be nomadic and our residence may be rented, but in heaven we will have a permanent residence, and our estate will be not for a period of years, but for eternity.

Not only are we assured that there are dwellings or rooms in the Father's house, thereby assuring us that although we will be one large family, we will not lose our individuality, but we are also assured that there are *many* of them, for there are many sons to be brought to glory. The Book of Revelation reveals that there are many citizens in the city, many subjects in the kingdom, many children in the household, many worshipers in the temple, and many angels, principalities, and powers in heaven; it will take "many homes" to house them all.

Some scholars do substantiate this concept. Bengel suggests, "By the plural number itself a variety of mansions seems also to be implied: for he does not say, a great mansion, but many mansions,"[2] while Godet remarks, "The image is derived from those vast oriental palaces, in which there is an abode not only for the sovereign and the heir to the throne, but also for all the sons of the king, however numerous they may be."[3]

Since Jesus did not elaborate any further on the subject, we dare not. The nature of this house, whether a massive palace or individual dwellings, is not revealed, and dogmatic speculation is unprofitable. But we are assured that it is where the Father lives, it is where Jesus lives, it is the home of the angels, and it is being prepared to house the redeemed sons of God who shall ascend with Christ in the Rapture. If Christ also inferred some spiritual principle in this state-ment, then so be it! Since the Hebrew word for "heavens" is in a dual voice, it is easy to believe that Jesus could well have used the literal Father's house as an illustration of spiritual truth, but an illustration is not an illusion; it is the applica-tion of fact to concept.

Jesus did not emphasize the "mansion"; He stressed that it was to be a "prepared place" where the redeemed would share His presence throughout eternity. He did not explain *how* the place in the Father's house would be prepared for them, but He promised that it *would* be prepared. God has never taken and will never take His people into an unprepared place. In Eden God first planted a garden and then placed man in it.

During the forty years of wandering in the wilderness, the ark of the Lord always went out before the camp, sometimes as much as three days' journey, to search for a new campsite (Numbers 10:33). And then, before leading Israel into Canaan, God assured her that there were vineyards, wells, and olive trees, "which thou plantedst not" (Deuteronomy 6:10–11). Better than any tour guide on Earth, God always has a place prepared before He leads His people onward. He is the perfect Shepherd who prepares the pasture before the sheep are brought into it.

Jesus knew better than any of us just what this preparation would entail, but in retrospect, we do realize that He had to go to the cross in order to procure the right for believers to enter heaven, and in His ascension He established that right. Reverend David Brown, DD, former professor of theology, Aberdeen, England, writes:

> "I go" or, according to what is undoubtedly the true reading, "because I go" (for the construction of the Greek) has decisive authority, and is inserted by all critical editors. The meaning is, "Doubt not that there is for all of you a place in My Father's house, for I am going on purpose to prepare it."[4]

Christ has done everything that was necessary to secure a welcome and a permanent place in heaven for His people. As our advocate, He preceded us to take possession for us and to secure our title. And, as Matthew Henry points out, "the happiness of heaven yet must be further fitted up for man.... Heaven would be an *unready* place for a Christian if Christ were not there."[5]

A new thing was about to take place: man brought into heaven! Man was not made for heaven, but for Earth, so Christ had to remake man. Equally true, heaven was not made for man, so heaven's citizens are being prepared for our arrival. There will be no strangeness when we enter the Father's house, for all of its inhabitants will have been prepared for man by Christ Jesus. Heaven is being prepared not to tolerate us but to *receive* us. We are not going to be special guests; we are citizens of that heavenly land. We will not be dependent upon heaven's graciousness to us; we will rest upon our rights as children of God.

But we will not have to exert those rights, for the Lord Himself is going to usher us into heaven. He assured His disciples, and us, "I will come again, and receive you unto myself; that where I am, there ye may be also" (John 14:3). Although the angels are commissioned to carry the dying believer to paradise, Jesus Christ our Lord will lead our triumphant entrance into the Father's house. At the coming of Christ, all believers, including those who have been awaiting His return in paradise, will receive their glorified bodies, which qualifies them to enjoy a more intimate relationship with God. Paul wrote:

> For if we believe that Jesus died and rose again, even so them also which sleep in Jesus will God bring with him.... For the Lord himself shall descend from heaven with a shout, with the voice of the archangel, and with the trump of God: and the dead in Christ shall rise first: then we which are alive and remain shall be caught up together with them in the clouds, to meet the Lord in

the air: and so shall we ever be with the Lord. Wherefore comfort one another with these words.

—1 THESSALONIANS 4:14, 16–18

Jesus will not send for us; He will come for us! And that
coming is not to lead us to a place that is better than life as
we have known it here on Earth but beneath the level of life
Christ Jesus enjoys. We are going to be brought to the same
Father's house that Jesus lives in—"that where I am, there ye
may be also" (John 14:3). The place that was due the Son of
God is the place that grace has given to the sons of God.
The Father's house is inseparable from the Father. It is not
merely owned by God; it is the residence of God. We shall
live with Him forever and ever. Who will care what form
these mansions have when we realize that God lives there
with us?

CHAPTER 4

Where Is It, and How Do We Get There?

S INCE THE BIBLE speaks so much about heaven, it must
mean something higher than these views. In the entire
Bible there are only thirteen books that do not mention
heaven; the other fifty-three all mention heaven in one way
or another. Six of the books that don't mention heaven are
in the Old Testament, and seven of them are in the New
Testament. Except for the Book of Numbers, these are very
short books with singular themes, and yet these themes are
harmonious with heaven.[1]

Heaven is heralded throughout the Bible, for the Bible
starts with God creating the heavens and ends with a
display of the new heaven—the New Jerusalem.

In the Hebrew text of the Old Testament, the most
generally used word for *heaven* is *shamayim*, which refers
to all space that is not occupied by the physical earth, from
the air we breathe to the vast expanse of space. Robert
Girdlestone says, "It is to be noticed that the form of the
word (*shamayim*) is neither singular nor plural, but dual.
This may be only an ancient form of the plural, but it is
supposed by some commentators to imply the existence of
a lower and an upper heaven, or of a physical and spiritual

heaven—'heaven and the heaven of heavens.'"[2]

It is fairly easy to trace this dualism throughout the Scriptures until, by the time we get into the Pauline epistles, such emphasis is laid upon the spiritual realm of heaven as to cause some to totally lose sight of the actual or physical heaven. The existence of the higher does not negate the reality of the lower, and generally heights are attained by climbing the lesser elevations.

THE VARIOUS LEVELS OF HEAVEN

The New Testament word for *heaven*, in the original Greek, is *ouranos*, and its meaning parallels the concept of the Hebrew word *shamayim*. Of the hundreds of times the word *heaven* appears in our Bibles, practically all of them are translations of these two words. Literally, they mean "the heights" and "that which is raised up." Throughout the Bible these words are used to delineate three separate areas. First, it speaks of the aerial heavens, or the atmospheric space that immediately surrounds the earth—the air we breathe and in which the birds fly and airplanes follow their schedules. It is the area in which our weather forms and functions.

These two words are also used when the Scriptures speak of the sidereal, or the celestial, heavens. The magnificent magnitude of the canopy of stars used to overwhelm the shepherd-king, inspiring David to write and sing, "The heavens declare the glory of God; and the firmament sheweth his handywork. Day unto day uttereth speech, and night unto night sheweth knowledge" (Psalm 19:1–2). "By the word of the LORD were the heavens made; and all the host of them by the breath of his mouth" (Psalm 33:6). With modern technology man is vastly expanding his knowledge of this realm of God's heavens.

But the most important use of these two words, in the original languages of the Scriptures, concerns the eternal dwelling place of God. It is this third usage that we are concerned with. The first heaven (the atmosphere) is the present abode of men. The second heaven (the sidereal heavens) is spoken of as the headquarters of Satan, but the third heaven is the residency of God Himself. This is what Paul means when he speaks of being caught up into "the third heaven" (2 Corinthians 12:2). It was from this third heaven that the Son of God descended to the earth to take on Himself the form of a man, and it was into this heaven that He ascended after His resurrection. It was from this third heaven that the Holy Spirit descended on the Day of Pentecost, and it is into this third heaven that the saints will ascend at the appearing of the Lord Jesus Christ.

Of course we realize that the Bible teaches us that the "heaven of heavens cannot contain" God (1 Kings 8:27), and we further understand that one of the essential attributes of God is His omnipresence; that is, He is present everywhere. Nevertheless, the Scriptures also positively declare that heaven is, in a particular way, the habitation of God:

> For thus saith the high and lofty One that inhabiteth eternity, whose name is Holy; I dwell in the high and holy place, with him also that is of a contrite and humble spirit, to revive the spirit of the humble, and to revive the heart of the contrite ones.
>
> —ISAIAH 57:15

Isaiah also cried, "Look down from heaven, and behold, from the habitation of thy holiness and thy glory" (Isaiah 63:15). Whenever David sought to express his thanks to God for deliverance from trouble, he used the title "God the Most

High." These statements cannot refer to God as being the highest of all gods, for repeatedly in Isaiah God is quoted as saying, "I am the first, and I am the last; and beside me there is no God" (Isaiah 44:6). The expression "most high" refers to the highest heaven, the "heaven of heavens" (Deuteronomy 10:14; Psalm 115:16), or the third heaven, God's eternal dwelling place. The reference is always to levels of abode and never to levels of gods.

A FAITH-GLIMPSE OF HEAVEN

One of the most difficult facets of faith is the time factor involved. God makes His promises in the scheduling of eternity, but man receives these promises in the span of time. Until a man is able to grasp the difference between these two dimensions, he cannot live in faith; he will walk by sight, or sense.

The eleventh chapter of Hebrews lists many Old Testament heroes of faith who were willing to look and long for God's promises whether they occurred in their lifetime or not. Notable among them is Abraham, of whom it is written, "He looked for a city which hath foundations, whose builder and maker is God" (Hebrews 11:10). This godly man left the greatest city the world had built up to that time to become a nomadic tent-dweller for the rest of his life, because God had told him of a God-designed, God-constructed city of a magnitude and splendor far beyond human imagination. Abraham never saw that city, but he never ceased looking for it, either. His excited anticipation of this promised possession was his to his dying day.

Many generations after Abraham's time, a vast number of faith-filled men and women, called "strangers and pilgrims on the earth" (Hebrews 11:13), also looked for this city.

The Bible records, "They desire a better country, that is, a heavenly: wherefore God is not ashamed to be called their God: for *he hath prepared for them a city*" (Hebrews 11:16, emphasis added).

David and the prophets also seemed to have caught a faith-glimpse of a heavenly city they called "Zion," and they extolled its beauties and glories. Consistently, men of faith have been made to anticipate heaven as a divinely built city.

Even the New Testament saints looked forward to a permanent and eternal residence in the form of a city. Jesus promised, "And if I go and prepare a place for you, I will come again, and receive you unto myself; that where I am, there ye may be also" (John 14:3). And in Hebrews we are told, "[We] are come…unto the city of the living God, the heavenly Jerusalem" (Hebrews 12:22). So the place Jesus promised to prepare for us is described by the inspired writer as "the city of the living God." As if to emphasize this concept, the writer further says, "Here have we no continuing city, but we seek one to come" (Hebrews 13:14). So the saints of all ages have anticipated heaven as a city—except the people of this generation, whose application of most of the Scriptures is very materialistic and humanistic, until they begin to think of heaven. Then they try to make exclusive spiritual application of what seems to be so clearly stated as a literal place—a city for heaven's residents to dwell in.

But since death is merely a change of where and how life is to be lived, there must be a place to accommodate our eternal life. Heaven is not made of thin air, nor is it merely a state of being. Although it will be far more blissful and glorious than our finite minds can now grasp, it will be real and very tangible. The Bible speaks of heaven being a place that is in contrast with the earth, which is an

unstable, insecure, and transitional place, while heaven is a
stable, secure, and eternal place. This contrast is made very
obvious in the New Testament summary of Abraham's life:

> By faith Abraham, when he was called to go out into
> a place which he should after receive for an inheri-
> tance, obeyed; and he went out, not knowing whither
> he went. By faith he sojourned in the land of promise,
> as in a strange country, dwelling in tabernacles with
> Isaac and Jacob, the heirs with him of the same
> promise: For he looked for a city which hath founda-
> tions, whose builder and maker is God.
> —HEBREWS 11:8–10

On Earth Abraham was a pilgrim on a pilgrim's journey,
living in a pilgrim's tent. But he had been promised a God-
planned, God-built city as permanent and unchanging as
God Himself.

An even stronger argument for heaven as a real locality
centers on our Lord Jesus Christ. At His birth in Bethlehem
of Judea He was given an earthly body exactly like ours,
except that the sin principle was not at work in it. After our
sins were vicariously imputed to Him and God's righteousness had extracted the death penalty at Calvary, He was
given a glorified body at His resurrection, and He ascended
into heaven in bodily form (Acts 1:9–11). In speaking of this,
Paul wrote, "When he [God] raised him [Christ] from the
dead, and set him at his own right hand in the heavenly
places, far above all principality, and power, and might, and
dominion, and every name that is named, not only in this
world, but also in that which is to come: And hath put all
things under his feet, and gave him to be the head over all
things to the church, which is his body, the fulness of him

that filleth all in all" (Ephesians 1:20–23).

This certainly locates Christ in a place of high honor in God's many-mansioned country. He ascended in corporeal form into a literal, real, identifiable place that is called heaven. As surely as His glorified body is a prototype of the body we shall have throughout eternity, so His present residence is a foretaste of that heavenly city the Holy Spirit has given us a taste for. "I go," Jesus said, "to prepare a place for you" (John 14:3). That speaks of locality, substance, something settled. This is the purpose of Christ's ascension; nothing could be simpler, more explicit, or more honest. Earth has been a place where we have been abiding; heaven will be the place where we will continue to abide. Each is real, each has been prepared by God, and each was the place of habitation for the sons of God. The major difference is in the degree of excellence and glory and in the closeness of our relationship to God.

Jesus left this earthly abode to enter heaven as a pioneer intent upon blazing a trail and preparing a place for us. He does not ask us to search for that trail; He has promised to backtrack and personally conduct us into heaven.

Through Moses, God promised Israel a land, but Israel did not have to pioneer the way or build cities or homes. They merely had to follow God's leader into Canaan and possess and enjoy the cities, houses, vineyards, and grain fields. So it is with us. We need only follow God's forerunner—Jesus— into a totally prepared place that already has everything we will ever need to sustain and fulfill our lives.

Edward M. Bounds, in writing of heaven, said:

> The future of the saint will not be impalpable and transitory, but defined, limited, real as soul and body will be real. The glorified will not be pilgrims, transient

visitors, or tenants at will, but settled, permanent, walled, established by title, through eternity by warranty deed, signed, sealed, recorded, possession given. No renters, no lessees of heaven, but all property and homeowners. Heaven's patent is issued to guarantee right and title. In fact, it is ours before we get there. It is reserved for us; it is guarded for us; our names of ownership are engraved, jeweled on our heavenly home....

All earthly houses, however beautiful, costly, and enduring they may be, are made with earthly hands and subject to decay. The marks of their death are on them, laid in their very foundations. The houses of heaven are God-built, and are as enduring and incorruptible as their builder. We will have bodies after the resurrection; transfigured they will be after the model of Christ's glorious body. The transfiguration will refine and spiritualize the substance of our bodies, but we will require houses then to locate us as now.

What houses they will be! They will be fitted essentially for every use, employment, and enjoyment of the heavenly citizens, worthy of God their builder, reflecting honor on and bringing glory to Him by the untold beauty, magnificence, grandeur of these God-built houses.[3]

These houses are not scattered indiscriminately throughout space; they are gathered together into a community to form a city. Just as Jesus promised, God has prepared our dwelling place in a most magnificent, beautiful, and commodious city that He calls the New Jerusalem—new in comparison with and in contrast to the old Jerusalem.

RELOCATING JERUSALEM

In his Gospel, John always uses the Greek word for Jerusalem, for it signified the political city, but in the Apocalypse he consistently uses the Hebrew name, the original and holier name. Paul makes this same distinction in his writing. This New Jerusalem is the fulfillment of everything for which the old Jerusalem was merely a figure.

From the days of David until Israel ceased to exist as a nation, the earthly Jerusalem was the capital city and the residence of the king. Ezra and Nehemiah, during the Babylonian captivity, envisioned the reconstruction of Jerusalem as synonymous with the reestablishment of the Jewish nation. In recent history we have observed the daring with which the Jews recaptured this old Jerusalem and the tenacity with which they hold on to it. It is, and always has been, the hub of the Jewish nation.

During the millennium, Jerusalem will again be the headquarters city for Christ's reign. It will be the central seat of government for the whole world. But with the passing of the old world and the coming of the new heavens and earth, the New Jerusalem will become the world's capital and will be the headquarters and residence of God. His throne will be there, His home is there, and His glory and His presence will be there, too. Just as David's presence gave Jerusalem a distinction above any other city in Israel, so the peculiar splendor of the New Jerusalem is the localized presence of God.

David's Jerusalem became the center of Jewish hopes. Their hearts were there; their songs eulogized the city; their prayers were directed toward it several times daily. When they were in captivity and away from it, they had no songs or prayers. "If I forget thee, O Jerusalem," the psalmist wrote, "let my right hand forget her cunning. If I do not remember thee, let my tongue cleave to the roof of my mouth; if I prefer not Jerusalem above my chief joy" (Psalm 137:5–6). Similarly, heaven has become the hope, the joy, and the excitement of the saints down through the ages, for the New Jerusalem will be the complete expression of everything the old Jerusalem exemplified: location, habitation, family, government, social joys, prosperity, security, continuity, and so on.

From the days of Christ through the pages of church history. this New Jerusalem has been the center of all Christians' hopes. It has calmed the fears of the persecuted, strengthened the courage of the martyrs, and impelled the missionaries to greater zeal. It really didn't matter what their circumstances were, because they had been promised residence in God's capital, the New Jerusalem. Temporal joys or hardships cannot be compared with the eternal provisions God has promised to the overcomer. Heaven will be worth it all.

This place is called the New Jerusalem not merely to form a contrast to the old Jerusalem, but because of its placement in God's time schedule. It does not come into view until the old heavens and the old earth have passed away and have been replaced with the new heavens and earth.

Will the New Jerusalem replace heaven?

Peter speaks of this exchange in his second epistle, where he writes, "But the day of the Lord will come as a thief in the night; in the which the heavens shall pass away with a great noise, and the elements shall melt with fervent heat, the earth also and the works that are therein shall be burned up" (2 Peter 3:10). In declaring that the heavens shall *pass away*, Peter does not mean a termination of existence or annihilation, for the Greek word he uses here is *parerchomai*, which means "to come near or aside."[4] In secular application, this word has been used in speaking of a ship passing through the sea, of a person passing from one place to another, and of events passing from the present into history. The main idea is *transition*, not *termination*.

Jesus used this same word when He said, "Heaven and earth shall pass away" (Mark 13:31), but He never taught the eradication of the earth or of mankind. Although strong language is used to describe the catastrophic upheavals that will occur during the final judgments—such as the earth "perishing" or the heavens being "dissolved"—the context of such passages will not allow us to interpret it as cessation. In speaking of the heaven and earth of Noah's time, Peter wrote, "The world that then was, being overflowed with water, perished" (2 Peter 3:6), but it was not the planet Earth that perished—only mankind and his world system. These were replaced by the progeny of Noah and a new system of life. So it will be in the final days, for God will purge the heavens and Earth from all vestiges of sin, and the evil world system will be replaced with a divine government. The earth, which has groaned under the curse God put on it as a punishment upon man, will be released from that curse and returned to God's blessing. The atmospheric heavens will no longer be the headquarters of the satanic kingdom, but will be the location of the New Jerusalem and the saints.

It will be a regeneration for creation just as the new birth has been a renewing for mankind: "Old things are passed away; behold, all things are become new" (2 Corinthians 5:17).

Since the Scriptures clearly teach that "the meek shall inherit the earth" (Psalm 37:9, 11, 29; Matthew 5:5) and that the righteous are to inhabit it forever (Isaiah 60:21; Romans 4:13), it surely must continue to exist forever. Furthermore, we are told that "the kingdoms of this world are become the kingdoms of our Lord, and of his Christ; and he shall reign for ever and ever" (Revelation 11:15). Christ's kingdom is frequently spoken of as an everlasting kingdom, so there must be perpetuity of Earth, mankind, society, and government, for how could Christ reign forever in a world that would someday cease to be?

Paul concluded his mighty doxology, "Unto him be glory in the church by Christ Jesus throughout all ages, world without end. Amen" (Ephesians 3:21). After the termination of this present eon, he contemplates many more eons of time stretching out into an unfathomable infinity. Surely eternal generations were provided for when God created the earth and instructed mankind to "be fruitful, and multiply, and replenish the earth" (Genesis 1:28), and since sin has not stopped any other program of God, we cannot assume that it has forced God to abandon this one either. God merely sent Christ Jesus to nullify the power of sin and to deliver mankind from the penalty of sin. Eventually God will completely eradicate all the effects of sin and restore man to the Edenic conditions in which he had his beginnings, for sin cannot destroy God's plan—God's plan destroys sin! When sin has been erased, then mankind will understand God's full salvation: man redeemed, the earth redeemed, the heavens redeemed, and a lost relationship redeemed.

THE TABERNACLE OF GOD WITH MEN

Although this consummated redemption will greatly change the earth's geography and political structure, life will go on; generations of people will follow generations, and society will be restructured to live harmoniously with one another and righteously before God. There will be no sin, no sickness, no pain, no death, no sorrow, and no devil. In comparison to the world we now know, it will be like "heaven." A purified earth, peopled with purified people, perpetually protected from satanic influence, would seem to be sufficient reward for God's faithful saints, but Jesus has not promised a perfected Earth to the overcomer; He pledged that "where I am, there ye may be also" (John 14:3). So when the Millennium has been completed, and the judgments have been executed, and the new heavens and the new earth have superseded the old, then, and not until then, will the New Jerusalem descend down from God to take its orbit over the earth. Then it will be said, "The tabernacle of God is with men, and he will dwell with them, and they shall be his people, and God himself shall be with them, and be their God" (Revelation 21:3).

William R. Newell, in his book on Revelation, says:

> But God's *home* is never spoken of until the New Jerusalem comes on the scene. Heretofore, it had been written: "Heaven is my throne, and the earth is my footstool" (Isaiah 66:1). To Israel in the wilderness, through Moses, Jehovah had indeed said, "Let them make me a sanctuary, that I may dwell among them," and it was done. Yet He dwelt in thick darkness, and judgments had to be executed from time to time upon that unbelieving and willful generation: so that finally, as we read in Ezekiel 8:6 (and in all the prophets) they drove Him away from His sanctuary—as they did afterwards His Son when He sent Him to them.
>
> But now all is over. Redemption has been accomplished—the thing dearest to God's heart— that which for all eternity reveals Him as Infinite. God is love, and yet absolutely righteous; *the Lamb slain* and now risen and abiding in that city,

becomes throughout the new creation the eternal proof and utterance of all God is![5]

This will complete the 360-degree turn that sin's detour forced upon mankind. From the beginning, God's "delights were with the sons of men" (Proverbs 8:31), and "the LORD taketh pleasure in his people" (Psalm 149:4).

Man was made not only in the image and likeness of God but also for God's pleasure (Ephesians 1:12; Colossians 1:16; Revelation 4:11). In Eden, God's man and man's God fellowshiped in the cool of the day, much as a father and son enjoy each other when day is done. How it must have broken the heart of God when sin separated Him from His earthly son. But God set His plan of redemption into immediate operation, looking forward to its culmination when sin would be forever erased and man could fully fellowship with his God again.

When the new heavens and the new earth have been completed, and God dares to move His many-mansioned dwelling place to Earth and invite His beloved bride to share His home, then the circle will have been completed. And once again God's eternal plan to be "with men" will be functional. The work of Christ who "suffered for sins...that he might bring us to God" (1 Peter 3:18) will be concluded, and He shall "present...to himself a glorious church, not having spot, or wrinkle, or any such thing; but that it should be holy and without blemish" (Ephesians 5:27). Then God will occupy Himself throughout eternity with the only creature the Bible ever declares that God loves—mankind!

It is interesting to note that after the New Jerusalem appears in Revelation 21, no mention is ever made of those glorious and eternal beings seen earlier in this book as surrounding the throne of God and of the Lamb. The concern is no longer with the cherubim, seraphim, living ones, or elders; God's throne has now been moved among men, and they are the objects of His affection and attention. It is not that these others have been replaced, for they are still there, completely ecstatic that God is now revealed to men in ways they could never know Him. These beings knew His eternity, His power, His holiness, and His glory, but redeemed men know God's love without limit, without partiality, and without deserving it. This divine love that was spurned in Eden and reaffirmed at Calvary will reunite man to his God in the New Jerusalem, for God's throne will be there, and man's home will be there. It will be the eternal resting place for both God and man: "Behold, the tabernacle of God is with men" (Revelation 21:3).

And what a marvelous and magnificent tabernacle it is! Its immensity, opulence, and beauty defy concise description, and even John's written record of his vision of this city strains man's imagination, for "eye hath not seen, nor ear heard, neither have entered into the heart of man, the things which God hath prepared for them that love him. But God hath revealed them unto us by his Spirit" (1 Corinthians 2:9–10).

Perhaps God's revelation through John can help us to crystallize our rather nebulous concepts of heaven as we see that it is actually a literal city designed by God, built by God, and inhabited by God and His people.

"How can I get to heaven?"

Our transfer from Earth to heaven may occur in one of two ways—through death or in the Rapture. Only those believers who are alive when Christ returns will go up in the Rapture. All others will enter heaven through the portals of death.[6]

There is only one way to heaven, and that is through Jesus Christ. He said:

> I am the way, the truth, and the life. No one comes to the Father except through Me. If you had known Me, you would have known My Father also; and from now on you know Him and have seen Him.
>
> —JOHN 14:6–7, NKJV

No one will enter heaven because he is a good person or due to his philanthropic works. (See Ephesians 2:8–9.) We have *all* sinned and fallen short of God's glory (Romans 3:23), and the price for living a sinful life is death (Romans 6:23). The good news is that God still loved us even though we were unlovable, and He sent His only Son to pay the price for our sinfulness (Romans 5:8). When we recognize, confess, and repent of our sinfulness, we receive God's forgiveness:

> If we confess our sins, he is faithful and just to forgive us our sins, and to cleanse us from all unrighteousness.
>
> —1 JOHN 1:9

Once the sin issue has been settled, we become new creatures in Christ Jesus—we live as new creatures. (See 2 Corinthians 5:17.) You ask, "Is it worth it to surrender my sinful ways and submit my life to the lordship of Christ?" Emphatically, yes! When we turn from sin, whether we view that sin as major or minor, we will receive a renewed hope of living eternally with Jesus, friends, and loved ones who have preceded us into heaven. Our death warrant, which has been served, no longer holds any power over our eternal destiny to live forever in the presence of God.[7]

CHAPTER 5

The New Jerusalem: Fact or Fiction?

N THE SAME terms, metaphors, and syntax that the Bible speaks of the earthly Jerusalem that is in Israel, it speaks of the New Jerusalem, the city of our God:

> Just as the old *earth* which disappeared was literal, and the new *earth* which takes its place is literal and substantial, *so also must the New Jerusalem be.*

It is a literal city because of the literalness of its description. If gold does not mean gold; nor pearls, pearls; nor precious stones, stones; nor exact measurements, real dimensions; then the Bible gives nothing accurate nor reliable. There is no one on earth who can assure your heart concerning the meaning of these "symbols"—if they are symbols! Nowhere in God's Word, for instance, is there any account of the "symbolism" of precious stones. Twelve such stones are found in the high priest's "four-square" breastplate (Exodus 28:15–21): sardius, topaz, carbuncle, emerald, sapphire, diamond, jacinth, agate, amethyst, beryl, onyx, jasper—"enclosed in gold in their settings. And the stones shall be according to the names of the children of Israel, twelve…like the engravings of a signet, every one according to his name, they shall be for the twelve tribes." No one doubts that these were literal stones, nor do we doubt that God has a special reason for assigning to each tribe a peculiar stone. Some time it may be revealed what these stones mean, and whether they have any connection with the foundations of the New Jerusalem; but to deny that they are literal stones in the Revelation, and to admit them as literal in Exodus, is not only absurd, but unbelieving.[1]

There just cannot be any doubt that this New Jerusalem is indeed a literal city. This heavenly city was the theme of the patriarchs' dreams and the inspiration for the drama of the poetic books. This city was prophesied by the prophets and proclaimed by Jesus, but it was not until John was on the isle of Patmos that any man was allowed even a glimpse of that city. In visions of Jesus Christ that God gave to John, he was allowed to see this New Jerusalem and was told that it was the Lamb's bride. This statement has caused many to spiritualize all that was shown about the city as man tries to make it describe the glorified saints who have become the bride of Christ. Their efforts are both futile and frustrating, for what John saw was the home of the bride before he saw the bride at home.

This is consistent with the way we often express ourselves. If I were describing my visit to a mutual friend, I might very well say: "As soon as I landed in Miami, I claimed my luggage, rented a car, and drove out to see Howard and Mae. When I located their address, I was pleasantly surprised to see their large Spanish design two-story house nestled amid tall palm trees and surrounded by a park-like yard. When I rang the doorbell, I was greeted with excited hugs and kisses, for I hadn't told them that I was coming."

It seems natural to speak of the place in which they live before speaking of the residents themselves, for that is the order in which I would experience it.

So it was with John. First he saw the residence of the bride, and then he saw the bride, but it was all one picture, one experience, one visit.

When Jesus spoke of heaven as "my Father's house," He assured us that it had "many dwelling places." Now John is allowed to see them from a distance. They form a city, a celestial city, with provision for every necessity and comfort of its citizens. It is bigger and brighter than any city men have ever built. It is radiant, resplendent, and restricted, but it is real—genuinely real and physically real, as opposed to spiritual reality.

This city described in Revelation 21 has all the elements of a city. It has specific dimensions; it has foundations; it has walls; it has gates; it has guards on the outside and inhabitants on the inside. It is called a city, the "holy city, New Jerusalem" (Revelation 21:2, NKJV), and, as we have seen, it also called the "Lamb's wife" (verse 9)—not because of those factors that make it a city, but because of the glorified, sanctified inhabitants who dwell in it. They are the bride, and the city is their home. Christ will not be married to a city, but the bride of Christ will enjoy living in this city. Here, in the Book of Revelation, the city and the bride are seen as an integrated whole, just as when we speak of a city we mean far more than concrete, buildings, lighting, and transportation. It takes people to make a city, and it takes buildings to house those people. Together they create a metropolis with a distinct personality and individuality.

The New Jerusalem is as literal a city as New York, Chicago, London, or Moscow, and it is as different from them as they are different from each other. For one thing, the New Jerusalem is of celestial origin. We have already seen that Abraham looked for a city that was designed and constructed by God (Hebrews 11:10), and John saw this city come down from God out of heaven (Revelation 21:1). What basis of comparison could we possibly make between the work of God, the master architect, and His most apt student among men? If man cannot compete with the delicate pattern of a snowflake or the suspension of a tree limb, how could one of his cities be compared to the one God has constructed for His saints?

God, who flung the countless stars into endless space, who spoke our world into existence, and who formed man with His own fingers, has built a city out of celestial materials and has kept it in His heavenly abode, far from the eyes of carnal man, just waiting to reveal it to the saints of the ages who will be its inhabitants.

Furthermore, this city of celestial design, origin, and materials has a unique location. It will not be situated on the earth but above the earth. Paul writes, "Jerusalem *which is above* is free" (Galatians 4:26, emphasis added), while John observes that "the nations…shall walk in the light of it" (Revelation 21:24). Very much as the cloud of fire rested above Israel's camp in her wilderness wanderings, this New Jerusalem will be above the earth in such perfect orbit as to become the source of light for the inhabitants of the earth below. From this orbital position the saints will have access to both the city above and the earth below, and the earth will have a constant awareness of the presence of God and His people. In addition to this, no activity on the earth will go undetected by the inhabitants of the New Jerusalem, for it will function very much as our spy satellites do now. This will greatly facilitate our role as administrators of God's authority and rule on the new earth.

WHAT IS THE SIZE OF THIS CITY?

While man may have the technology to suspend a space station in orbit above Earth's atmosphere, such an object isn't large enough to be even a scale model of God's New Jerusalem. This suspended city is more than large—it is gigantic. Well, at least it is monstrous by our standards of comparison, but I suppose that in God's eyes it is miniature, for God tends to do things on a very large scale. Consider His sidereal heavens. As man has developed more and more powerful instruments with which to explore the myriad stellar systems around us, he has discovered more and more of these systems. It now seems that space is an endless expanse of galaxy after galaxy of God's handiwork.

Even in the creation of God's angelic servants, the Word speaks of an incalculable number of them, and when God created man, He did so on an expanding pattern of reproduction that now seems to be multitudinous. Usually God's "normal" is viewed by us as a "miracle." His proportions, patterns, and provisions are so far beyond us that He explains, "For as the heavens are higher than the earth so are my ways higher than your ways" (Isaiah 55:9).

Since this is so, we would expect that any city God built would be colossal. And it is! We are told that the city is a cube 12,000 furlongs in each dimension: length, breadth, and height (Revelation 21:16). Since a furlong is 582½ feet (or approximately one-eighth of a mile), this translates to 1,500 miles in all directions. If this city were set on United States territory, it would extend from the northernmost tip of Maine to the southernmost point of Florida, and it would reach from the Atlantic Ocean to the Colorado River. If it were placed over the European countries it would cover all of England, France, Germany, Italy, eastern Europe, and half of Russia.

In Jonah's day Nineveh was considered a massive city, for we are told that Jonah had barely begun to enter it after traveling a full day's journey beyond the outside walls. But by comparison, this heavenly city would make Nineveh look like a small housing development. Imagine a city 1,500 miles from city limit to city limit. There are few countries in the world that exceed these dimensions of 2,250,000 square miles.

But that is only the measurement of the first level, for John declared that the city was as high as it was wide. It is not a square; it is a cube. Imagine a high-rise apartment building or a skyscraper that was 1,500 miles tall—but this is an entire city built layer upon layer, mile after mile, to this total height.

Since we are specifically told that there are streets in this city, let's assume that they are laid out on a square grid at one-mile intervals (which is far less frequent than in any city on Earth). This grid would give us 3,000 streets per level, each one 1,500 miles long for a total street length of 4,500,000 miles per level. If we assume that each level of this New Jerusalem will be one mile above the preceding level, there could be as many as 1,500 of these levels, thereby giving the city over 6,750,000,000 miles of roads—all made with pure gold.

Even the jasper walls that surround the first level are either one-half mile high or wide, whichever dimension is meant. The foundation that would be required for a city of this mass, built of gold, would have to be so strong that nothing on Earth would do. The very weight of the New Jerusalem would crush the crust of our globe, so God chose to hang the city in space, just as He has suspended all of His worlds.

In order to scale down the magnitude of such a mammoth city, some writers have suggested that it is in the shape of a pyramid, while others say it is only square with a very high mountain in the middle of it. But John, who saw it, said it was a cube (Revelation 21:16), and I would rather trust the word of an eyewitness than the theory of a skeptic.

WHY IS THE NEW JERUSALEM SO LARGE?

I must admit that these dimensions for a city stagger the imagination, but everything God has ever done has been beyond our belief until some man was able to see it either by faith or by fact. John did not write from a concept of faith but from the experience of participation. He was there. He watched it being measured and recorded the figures for the rest of us.

But why is heaven so large? When God created this world we now live in, "he formed it to be inhabited" (Isaiah 45:18). Surely, then, He would not lavish all this splendor and spaciousness upon this eternal city without knowing that sufficient numbers of men would embrace His salvation to fill it. Is it not likely that our concept of the redemptive program of God is too small? We tend to overemphasize the "little flock" concept and almost automatically take the position of being a minority group. But God has built a permanent residence for His redeemed people that could accommodate nearly twenty-eight billion people if each resident were given a quarter mile of territory, and certainly no city would have lots this large.[2] Assuming four lots per square mile, this would give each piece of property over 2,500 feet of depth and a total of nearly 7 million square feet. Here on Earth, any area that has less than five people per square mile is considered nearly uninhabited. Even barren Iceland boasts fifty-five persons per square mile; some of our more densely populated areas, such as Malta, have over twenty-six hundred people per square mile; both the Netherlands and South Korea have about nine hundred fifty persons per square mile. In calculating heaven's potential at only four persons per square mile, we're grossly understating its capacity. If heaven is to be populated as the Netherlands now is, it would have over thirty trillion (30,000,000,000,000) people!

This city isn't large in order to accommodate the angels; they will continue to live in the Father's house where the New Jerusalem was constructed. It isn't this big to take care of ten billion years of procreation, for Christ stated that in heaven we will be as sexless as the angels—there will be no procreation there.

At the end of the Millennium, after Satan is cast into the lake of fire and the unrighteous dead are raised, judged, and also cast into this lake that burns with fire forever and ever, the new heaven and earth replace the old. Then this marvelous and mammoth New Jerusalem will descend down from God's abode to take its place in orbit over this world. There will be far more people who have been ransomed and redeemed by the blood of Jesus Christ than we have expected, and there will be room enough for all of them.

God's goal was to have fellowship with man. He made man in His image. Sin destroyed that fellowship, but God's plan didn't change. God still desires fellowship. No work of God has ever failed, and His program of redemption won't be a failure either.

WHAT WILL THIS CITY BE LIKE FOR ITS CITIZENS?

Early in the Book of Revelation John saw "a great multitude, which no man could number, of all nations, and kindreds, and people, and tongues...before the throne, and before the Lamb, clothed with white robes, and palms in their hands; and [they] cried with a loud voice, saying, Salvation to our God which sitteth upon the throne, and unto the Lamb" (Revelation 7:9–10). Now this multitude has a home, for heaven has been built to the dimensions necessary to properly house the number of inhabitants that God is expecting, and that is an innumerable throng, all of whom are members of God's family.

Heaven is not a solitary, fleecy cloud where a saint will play harp solos; it is a city filled with happy people busily engaged in the activities of God and enjoying social fellowship with other members of the family.

CHAPTER 6

What Will the New Jerusalem Be Like?

N O CHAMBER OF commerce on Earth has ever written a brochure that comes close to describing how livable heaven will be. Bombarded as we are by sex, crime, violence, inflation, and insecurity, it is healthy to turn our minds from the unlovely to meditate on that which is lovely. Paul wisely wrote, "Finally, brethren...whatsoever things are lovely...think on these things" (Philippians 4:8). This injunction is as apropos to our generation as it was to Paul's generation.

Even taking time to look at a flower can flush the mind of much tension; viewing a snowcapped mountain or gazing into the depths of the Grand Canyon can bring a sense of deep inner tranquility and peace. A glimpse of the beautiful does for the human spirit what a recharge does for a storage battery: it becomes a renewing of life, a regeneration of energies.

All the excitement, variety, and activity of a major city will be there, but with none of the negatives. The dreams and ambitions of thousands of immigrants who have excitedly viewed the Statue of Liberty in New York Harbor will more than be fulfilled for the pilgrims and strangers who enter the

New Jerusalem as its citizens. Whether enjoying the thrill of a symphony, the fulfillment of a job well done, or the relaxation of an afternoon in the park, all of the inhabitants of this beautiful city will find it more than satisfactory. It will afford protection, provision, and pleasure never obtained in any earthly city. Its food and fellowship will exceed anything that earthly kings have ever enjoyed. It is inconceivable to imagine any lack in this city. It will not be an inadequate or a lonely place; it is, as we will see, a very lovely place. It is tailor-made by God for His special redeemed people who have become the peculiar object of the divine love.

WHY IS THERE SO MUCH EXTRAVAGANCE?

What it must have done to John when the Spirit took him to that giant mountain and gave him a view into the New Jerusalem! What exquisite beauty, what entrancing symmetry, what magnificent magnitude he saw. Nothing on Earth could adequately compare with it. It was the "heavenly Jerusalem" (Hebrews 12:22), designed and built by God (Hebrews 11:10) of heavenly materials so superior and beautiful that the earth has only rare deposits of any of them. No explorer or mountain climber has viewed such a breathtaking scene as John did, and since he was commanded to write and describe what he saw to the best of his anointed abilities, we have been given a vicarious view into the beauties that God has prepared for us.

After poetically describing Jesus as superior to anything known on this earth, the writer summed it up by saying, "He is altogether lovely" (Song of Solomon 5:16). If He is lovely, or beautiful, then surely His home must be exquisite beyond comprehension. And it is! Gold is used more lavishly than we use concrete or bricks; valuable gemstones form the foundations of the city, and its gates are elegant pearls. It is, as we have already seen, immense, but it is equally elegant. There is nothing that is beautiful in the eyes of God that will not be part of His great city, and He has promised to share this city as the home of His bride. Look at it.

John writes:

> In the spirit, he took me to the top of an enormous high mountain and showed me Jerusalem, the holy city, coming down from God out of heaven. It had all the radiant glory of God and glittered like some precious jewel of crystal-clear diamond. The walls of it were of a great height, and had twelve gates; at each of the twelve gates there was an angel, and over the gates were written the names of the twelve tribes of Israel.... The city walls stood on twelve foundation stones, each one of which bore the name of one of the twelve apostles of the Lamb.
>
> —REVELATION 21:10–14, JB

From a vantage point atop an exceedingly tall mountain John was given a glimpse of the outside of the city in Revelation 21 and of the inside in Revelation 22. Some have suggested that this mountain was inside the city itself, but John could not have viewed the walls, foundations, and gates of the city from within. God merely used this mountain as a viewing platform for John.

His first impression was that the city actually glowed with the glory of God. Knox translates that the city was "clothed in God's glory" in verse 11 of chapter 21. In trying to describe this glory, John says, "Her brilliance sparkled like a very precious jewel with the clear light of crystal" (Revelation 21:11, PHILLIPS), and while the King James translators call the stone jasper, the Jerusalem Bible calls it a diamond. No one has accurately described the glory of God, for Earth has few things with which to compare it. The Old Testament refers to this glory as a cloud, as incense, as a fire, and as a radiant light, but John says the entire city had the fire, sparkle, depth of beauty, and flashing spectrum of a giant diamond in brilliant light. In describing the throne of God, John recorded, "A throne was set in heaven, and one sat on the throne. And he that sat was to look upon like a jasper and a sardine stone: and there was a rainbow round about the throne, in sight like unto an emerald" (Revelation 4:2–3). Now John uses the same phrases to describe the city in which this throne will have eternal residence. It sparkles like a gemstone and produces a display of light that reveals every color of the rainbow. Man has attempted to create this effect with his flashing electric lights and colored, gas-filled tubes, but the very material out of which this city is built catches the radiant glory of God and reflects it in continually changing hues of pure color that sparkle like a diamond.

Any who have observed the fascination with which a young lady plays with her first diamond under a bright light will have a picture of the delight God's radiant glory will give to its inhabitants. It will be expanding, enveloping, ever-changing, enchanting, and endless. The visual joy of this displayed glory of God will make heaven an enviable place to spend eternity. To whatever extent our visual senses can stand this stimulation, heaven will excite us completely. There will be no need for psychedelic substitutes; God's glory will more than suffice.

WHAT ABOUT THE WALLS OF THE CITY?

From the mountaintop John seems to have had a clear view of the walls that surround this radiant city, and his first impression was that they were very large (Revelation 21:12). In giving us the dimensions of these walls in verse 17, John says that the angel measured it in cubits of a man, which was the standard Old Testament measure taken from the king's elbow to the tip of his longest finger. It varied from 18 to 22 inches. This would give us a dimension of 216 to 240 feet. But he doesn't specify whether this measurement applies to the height or the width of the walls. Scholars are divided in their opinions. The King James translators and later revisers leave it to the reader to determine. The Living Bible declares, "Then he measured the thickness of the walls and found them to be 216 feet *across*...," while the Jerusalem Bible declares, "He measured its wall, and this was a hundred and forty-four cubits *high*...," so we cannot speak with any certainty. Nonetheless, it is difficult to believe that John would consider walls 240 feet tall as "great and high" (verse 12) in comparison to a city that was 1,500 miles high. It is easier to believe that he was impressed with their thickness than with their height. But either way, these are huge walls, sufficiently tall and strong to protect the inhabitants of the city.

But John isn't the only one who saw these six thousand miles of walls. Isaiah got a glimpse of the church in her final glory and gave us some spiritual insight into this glorious city. He said, "The glory of Lebanon shall come unto thee...to beautify the place of my sanctuary; and I will make the place of my feet glorious" (Isaiah 60:13). From the depths of the mountains was to come material that would beautify God's dwelling place, and John says this material was jasper and that the walls were of such a clear jasper as to be like crystal. Some translators refer to it as diamond. (See Revelation 21:11 in the Jerusalem Bible.) Since jasper was used as a descriptive comparison for God seated on the throne (Revelation 4:3), whatever these walls are, they become a constant reminder of God himself. In Isaiah's description he declares, "Thou shalt call thy walls Salvation" (Isaiah 60:18). Certainly God is not only our savior; He has become our salvation (Revelation 7:10; 12:10), and throughout eternity we will be surrounded by walls of salvation that forever protect our rights to salvation and our security from intrusion. Now we know constant pressure from sin and Satan, but then we will be walled in with God. Now we are assailed by doubts and fears about our deliverance from sin, but then it will be a settled issue once and for all. Now we live surrounded by sin, but then we will live surrounded by salvation. Isaiah declared, "In that day shall this song be sung in the land of Judah; we have a strong city; salvation will God appoint for walls and bulwarks" (Isaiah 26:1). Even viewed from the mountain peak outside the city, these walls evoke a song of praise. Indeed, saints, we have a strong city; its mighty walls are our eternal salvation. Once inside those walls, we will forever be shut away from sin, Satan, and sickness, and we will be shut in with God, the saints, and the angels. We will be home at last, thoroughly enjoying the security, comfort, and affection that home affords.

But, of course, stone walls need strong foundations, and John saw not only strength in the foundation stones but also beauty and value, for John saw the foundation garnished, or faced, with costly gems of nearly unbelievable size and beauty. A. C. Gaebelein describes the foundation like this:

The Jasper again stands first; the wall itself is of Jasper, while the first foundation stone mentioned is also Jasper. It stands for the Glory of God. Then the stones follow in their order. The Sapphire (blue); the Chalcedony (a combination of grey, blue and yellow); the Emerald (green); the Sardonyx (a pale blue); the Sardius (blood red); the Chrysolite (purple and green); the Beryl (bluish green); the Topaz (pale green or golden); the Chrysoprasus (mixed blue, green and yellow); the Jacinth (combination of red, violet and yellow); and the Amethyst (purple). And what must be the deeper meaning all these precious stones! What varied aspects of the Glory of God they must represent! And the redeemed in their heavenly city shall know, understand and enjoy it all. What wonderful, unspeakable glory is ahead of us![1]

Adam Clark reminds us, "These stones are nearly the same with those on the breastplate of the high priest, Exodus 28:17–21, and probably were intended to express the meaning of the Hebrew words there used."[2] But while the stones may be the same, their representation changed, for the names of the twelve tribes of Israel were engraved on the stones in the breastplate, but John says that "the wall of the city had twelve foundations, and in them the names of the twelve apostles of the Lamb" (Revelation 21:14). The breastplate stones were for the Old Testament believers, while the foundation stones are the New Testament apostles. Paul wrote, "[We] are built upon the foundation of the apostles and prophets, Jesus Christ himself being the chief corner stone; in whom all the building fitly framed together groweth unto an holy temple in the Lord" (Ephesians 2:20–21).

But whatever their meaning may be, we cannot mistake

the scintillating beauty of these stones, and what mammoth stones they are! If it takes only twelve of them to face this six-thousand-mile foundation, then each stone must be about five hundred miles long. There is no place on Earth where such a stone could be found, for these stones, merely the size of hen's eggs, would cost a man's life savings here on Earth. But this city was not constructed on Earth or of earthly materials. It was built in God's heaven by the hand of the Creator of the earth, for whom securing materials is no problem.

Looking from the top to the bottom of this wall, John saw radiance, brilliance, and color that defied description. Heaven will not be colorless and bleached, but colorful and bright.

Years ago while ministering in South Korea, the pastor of the Presbyterian church in which I was preaching summed up his impression of his recent trip to America by saying, "I couldn't get over the brilliant colors in America. Your houses, cars, clothes, and even your stores are of such brilliant and varied hues that they stood out in marked contrast to my country." If America enjoys the pleasure of color because of her limited relationship to God, how greatly will the saints enjoy color when they are shut in with God forever! Earth's transitory rainbow will eternally adorn the foundation of the wall in the form of gemstones that never fade or lose their luster. And this is only the foundation; imagine what the houses are like!

Still, walls, however beautiful, would cease to be protective and would become prohibitive if there were no openings in them—just ask any penitentiary inmate. The walls of God's great city have twelve costly gates in them, three to each wall. This is the way the early city of David was built, for it allowed maximum entrance and exit for the inhabitants of the city. But David's gates were built of iron while God's gates are made of solid pearls. One pearl forms each gate (Revelation 21:21). While we are not given any dimensions for these gates, they must be enormous since there are only three to each wall, leaving 375 miles between the gates (assuming that they are placed equidistant around the wall). Imagine twelve giant pearls, large enough to control the flow of traffic for city of *3,375,000,000* cubic miles, which, A. S. Worrell declares, would provide more than nine quadrillion rooms 30 feet long, 30 feet wide, and 30 feet high, even if we allowed half of the area for streets.[3]

In the times when John wrote, pearls held the highest rank among precious stones, so John saw man's most valuable treasure being used for gates. Isaiah said that these gates would be called "Praise" (Isaiah 60:18), which is consistent with the way we have been taught to enter God's presence: "Enter into his gates with thanksgiving, and into his courts with praise" (Psalm 100:4). Gaebelein reminds us that "the pearl is a type of church. She is the one pearl of great price for which the Lord gave all he had (Matthew 13:45–46)."[4]

If we accept typology, the pearl gates would represent the church, while the open gateway itself would speak of the twelve tribes of Israel, since each gate had the name of one tribe inscribed above it (Revelation 21:12). This is a beautiful example of the interrelationship between the Old Testament saints and the New Testament believers.

Furthermore, John tells us that each gate had an angel as guard (Revelation 21:12) since the gates will be open perpetually (verse 25). Isaiah calls these guards "watchmen": "I have set watchmen upon thy walls, O Jerusalem, which shall never hold their peace day nor night" (Isaiah 62:6).

So the foundation stones typify the New Testament apostles, while the gates are named for the twelve tribes in the Old Testament. The gates themselves speak of the church of Christ, while the angel guards are part of the great host of spiritual beings who have never known the sting, stench, and power of sin. But now there is no separation among them; together these created beings of God, both of heavenly and earthly origin, form the outer walls of the lovely New Jerusalem. How precious is this picture of God uniting us all into one.

Revelation 21:21 tells us that these gates lead into the main streets of the city that are made of pure gold so as to seem to be crystal clear. It has been my privilege to travel to many of the countries of this world and to visit their most illustrious cities. But no matter how magnificent the city, I have observed that they are willing to use cobblestones, asphalt, or concrete for their roadways—august materials for their buildings, but abject materials for their roads. But not heaven. Its buildings and its roads are all built of the finest gold imaginable (verses 18, 21).

Try to imagine the excitement of walking on the lower level of heaven and looking straight up through fifteen hundred levels of pure gold streets, all sparkling as crystal, strong and glorious—incalculable tons of gold, worth billions of dollars by today's monetary standards. Then look around you and behold majestic mansions and magnificent houses as far as the eye can see, all made of this same highly purified gold. It is, indeed, a crystal city with nothing to hinder the flow of light and color. Everything is constructed of durable materials; nothing that could decay, rot, mold, or rust is used here, for this city will endure eternally.

WHAT IS THE RIVER OF LIFE?

As John shifted his gaze from the lovely construction of the city to its living conditions, the first thing that caught his attention and imagination was the great flowing river: "And he shewed me a pure river of water of life, clear as crystal, proceeding out of the throne of God and of the Lamb" (Revelation 22:1). To John, who had lived his life in the arid, burning East and was familiar with the long lines of women carrying water pots on their heads to and from a well or spring of water, the sight of such a lavish water supply flowing within the city itself was amazing. One of the most precious commodities on Earth is water, for it matters not what else you have—if you have no water, life will not linger very long. Whole civilizations have perished for lack of water, but heaven's supply is so vast there will never be a rationing program.

One of the first things we are told about Adam's Eden is that a river went out of it to water the garden and then parted and flowed in four separate channels (Genesis 2:10). God woke into existence a creation that was specific for man's needs, but water was necessary for it to continue to replenish itself. So God supplied an abundant amount of water.

When we read Ezekiel's vision of the great temple, which many believe speaks of the millennial reign of Christ, we also see a river that flows from the throne of God (Ezekiel 47:1–12). As the waters were measured, Ezekiel was urged to walk out into greater and greater depths of the river. At first it was only ankle deep; then knee deep, thigh deep, shoulder deep, and, finally, water of such depth that he could swim in it but so wide he could not swim across it. Both John and Ezekiel saw a more than sufficient water supply for God's people.

Trying to understand this heavenly river has given concern to some commentators on the Scriptures. Some have felt that in prophetic language the term "waters" always refer to the peoples of the earth, and so they try to make this river symbolic of the many people who will be in heaven. But they admit that nowhere else in Scripture do we see people issuing from the throne of God. Others try to make this river a picture of water baptism and seek to create a deep spiritual experience for their candidates as though the waters with which or into which they are being baptized actually came from God's throne. Still others spiritualize this river as the grace of God that comes to man through the preaching of the gospel, while some simply make it the giving of peace to the troubled nations. A few merely pass it off as Eastern imagery describing happiness and plenty.

But what John saw was only an earthly image of something that is gloriously spiritual. It is a natural river of supernatural properties. This river does not belong to the earth or to earthly people in any way whatsoever. The river is a heavenly river; it belongs to the heavenly city, and it is for the use and joys of the heavenly citizens. There is not one indication in the entire Bible that this river flows down out of the New Jerusalem to the inhabitants of this earth. These are literal waters of a quality that answers to the distinctive character of God's holy city. These waters, unlike the earth's mixture of hydrogen and oxygen, are a corresponding reality to the Lamb and to the city. They are as real as the Lamb is real, as genuine as the streets, as authentic as the walls, and as actual as the city itself. The psalmist prophetically sang of this river, "There is a river, the streams whereof shall make glad the city of God, the holy place of the tabernacles of the most High" (Psalm 46:4), while Ezekiel swam in it and John saw it flow. It is a real river, and what a river it is!

In Revelation 22:1 John described the river as "clear as crystal," "bright as crystal" (RSV), or "sparkling like crystal" (NEB, PHILLIPS). It flows like a living, liquid diamond, catching the rays of God's glory and reflecting them in a dazzling array of rainbow colors. Those testimonies of seeing into heaven that I have heard or read all declare that this river is beautiful beyond description. It not only gives life—it *is* life. It not only gives off the colors that a pure crystal would reflect, but it also resounds with the most beautiful music imaginable. (Remember that here on Earth we have used crystal as the receiving agent for radio waves for many years.) The combination of flowing water, sparkling colors, and beautiful music have long been used to produce pleasant, sensual sensations. How marvelous it will be to have this so perfected and purified as to enable us to respond in the highest form of joy, pleasure, and delight with no erotic or carnal overtones. Like innocent children, we will experience gaiety without guilt, enjoyment without exhaustion, and pleasure without pain. This crystal river will give the saints visual, aural, and sensory pleasure as a by-product to being the source of life for all the inhabitants of the New Jerusalem.

David said that the fountainhead of this river was God Himself: "And thou shalt make them drink of the river of thy pleasures. For with thee is the fountain of life" (Psalm 36:8–9). John agreed by declaring that this river "flowed from the throne of God and of the Lamb" (Revelation 22:1, PHILLIPS). These waters are the issuing life of the throne, just as the city is the embodiment of God's glory. This throne is the throne of the Father and of the Son, and this river "flowing from the throne" (TLB) is the reviving and all-animating life and spirit of all this embodiment of deity in that sublime city. Not only is the Lamb the light of this heavenly city; He is also the life of its inhabitants, flowing forth abundantly to minister to the residents of the New Jerusalem.

Joseph A. Seiss suggests that this river "is the Holy Ghost for that celestial tabernacle, as God and the Lamb are the temple of it. It is the divine emanation from the Father and the Son that fills and cheers and forever rejoices the dwellers in that place....It is the Spirit of Glory which they drink and embody; and it is for their pleasure and blessed-ness, as to no other class of the human family."[5] In a very elementary way we might say that this river is God in liquid form—God in a configuration we can consume and assimi-late. This is not too inconsistent with the operation of the Holy Spirit in this generation of believers, for He brings the things of God to believers and makes them to become spiri-tual life and refreshment. But even the greatest anointings men have experienced on Earth will be beneath compar-ison with the unmingled purity, heavenliness, and glorious fullness that will be constantly available to all of heaven's inhabitants. In Adam's Eden, God provided a water system whereby the moisture came up through the ground to water the plant life. Similarly, God is now watering the spiritual earth, His church. While He does promise (through the prophet Joel) seasonal rains, He also promises (through the prophet Hosea) the daily dew. The church is kept alive, invigorated, refreshed, and growing by the action of the Holy Spirit coming up through the earth, or the humanity of the members of the church. That is why we are encouraged to cry, "Spring up, O well..." (Numbers 21:17), and why Jesus declared, "He that believeth on me, as the scripture hath said, out of his belly shall flow rivers of living water" (John

7:38). In our limited dimension of time and space, the Spirit flows through human instrumentality up through flesh. This explains why we hear some speakers and are unmoved, while other speakers refresh our spirits and renew our faith.

Some have learned to get a well springing up in their lives. They have learned the secret of flowing God's Spirit out to others. Others are dependent upon a water course from another. But in the holy city there will be no secondary medium through which the Spirit ministers to people. We will not be dependent upon whatever life flow we can get from one another. Down here, no matter how hard we try to be pure channels, there is always a tainting because of our personality, faith level, bias, or pride. We can't totally help it; this is part of the weakness of our flesh.

But there is coming a day when the moving of the Spirit will not be hindered or shaded by any man's theology, methods of operation, prejudiced concepts, or lack of understanding. The river will flow directly from God to His people, and they will drink of the spirit of grace and glory without having it come through the earthly form of flesh. The life of God and His Son will roll as a crystal river, giving forth God's exhaustless blessedness direct from the throne with neither the need nor limitation of an agency.

When evangelist Loren Fox was caught away in vision form to view this eternal city, he said the angel that conducted his tour explained that everyone who entered this city for the first time had to submerge himself in its waters until all earthliness was dissolved from his spirit and soul. Since he was there only on a visit, he was not allowed to enter the river; he passed over it into the city.[6]

But others have written about the blessedness of being in this river and of the peace that flowed into their souls as they relaxed in its waters. They have told of absorbing great strength and vitality from its waters and of finding depths of fellowship with others who relaxed in its waters, very much as people on Earth go to hot springs or health spas and socialize while relaxing in the refreshing waters.

All of the joys, strengths, blessings, and life forces of heaven are renewable assets, for this great river revitalizes the life of heaven's citizens. It is, John says, a river of life, and, unlike earthly rivers, it has no harmful pollutants, unpleasant odors, and never an unpalatable taste. It doesn't rise from any dark cave in the earth, as does Israel's Jordan, nor does it grow from additions of other little streams. It is a fully developed river the moment it issues from its source in God's throne. It has no windings, stagnations, or obstructions, nor is it dependent upon clouds to replenish its waters. It is never muddy because of its banks, and it never rises or falls according to the seasons of the year. It is an availability of God's life, glory, and nature that insistently and consistently flows through this vast city, beautifying, invigorating, and lifting everything that it contacts. Joseph A. Seiss says, "The life it symbolizes, and is, and gives, is divine life, the life of the throne of God and of the Lamb, the life that rolls forth in the highest fulness from its living source, pellucid as the city which it supplies, and as unfailing and all-gladdening as the Spirit of holiness itself. O the blessedness of the eyes that see and the people who enjoy this river of God—these crystal waters of eternal life."[7]

This river flows down the center of the broad, golden streets of the New Jerusalem (Revelation 22:2), and on each side of the river grow rows of the trees of life. The Jerusalem Bible translates this verse, "On either side of the river were the trees of life, which bear twelve crops of fruit in a year, one in each month, and the leaves of which are the cure for the pagans." What a beautiful sight it must be! I have visited a few cities that had a narrow row of trees down the center of its streets, such as the waterways of Amsterdam. But in heaven we have a great river bounded by tree-lined parks that form the median strip for the roadway, perhaps offering one-way traffic on each side of the river. Nothing I have ever seen on Earth could begin to compare with this 1,500-mile-long (minimum) parkway that forms the main avenue of heaven.

WHAT IS THE TREE OF LIFE?

The first paradise (Adam's Eden) was decorated with trees, and among them was the tree of life (Genesis 2:9). Students of the Hebrew language tell us that this refers to a species of trees, just as we speak of the oak tree, the apple tree, or the pecan tree. Very likely there were many trees of this one species in the garden. Unlike the tree of the knowledge of good and evil, which was prohibited (Genesis 2:17), the tree of life was provided to maintain Adam's life on the face of the earth. Some writers say that Adam did not eat of the tree, because he eventually died. However, it seems far more consistent with the Genesis account that he did, in fact, eat regularly of this tree. God shut him out of the garden lest he continue to eat of the tree and live after sin had separated him from God and had brought defilement into his moral and physical nature. What a curse it would have been for Adam to live perpetually in his fallen state. When he no longer had access to the tree of life, he began to die. It took a long time for the effects of the tree to wear off, though, for Adam lived 930 years. What a powerful life source that tree must have been.

And what a perpetual life source that tree will be to us when we get to heaven. Wherever the river of life flows, the tree of life grows, offering its varied fruit for both our enjoyment and endurance. This species of tree is more than a symbol of life; it is the support of life. It is the life of God made available in a food form. On Earth, water and food are paired essentials for the sustenance of human life, and in the New Jerusalem these prime necessities will still be accessible together.

During the church age this life of God has been symbolized in two ways. Jesus said, "Except ye eat the flesh of the Son of man, and drink his blood, ye have no life in you. Whoso eateth my flesh, and drinketh my blood, hath eternal life; and I will raise him up at the last day" (John 6:53–54). This, of course, is symbolic language teaching us that we must be regular partakers of Christ in order to have divine life functioning, but it is put in the figure of eating and drinking. The ritual that is generally associated with this teaching is called "the Lord's table" (1 Corinthians 10:21) and "the Lord's supper" (1 Corinthians 11:20). It is an eating and drinking together with one another and with God.

This tree of life is also made available, in a very embryonic form, to the church as the "fruit of the Spirit" (Galatians 5:22–23). These nine fruit of the Spirit make available to the saints on Earth a small measure of the character and graces of God's divine nature. The fruit is more beneficent to others than to the one who bears it. In other words, the Christian who allows this fruit to develop in his life is gaining his life source from the Spirit of God within, while others are receiving the blessings of that life by partaking of the outer fruit of his altered life.

INDESCRIBABLE BEAUTY

Over the years I have talked with several who have had near-death experiences that brought them to a point where they too caught a glimpse of the New Jerusalem. As I wrote this book on heaven, several took the time to phone, send tapes, or write me letters describing visions they had of this city of God. One thing the visions all had in common: the city is beautiful beyond description. Some were overwhelmed by the beauty of the building materials, as was John. Others were more enthralled with the nature of the light that seems to produce a sensorial experience as well as a visual one. Still others remembered the overall symmetry and design of the city as being extremely pleasing. But all admitted that Earth has little with which to compare it. Our vocabulary is too limited, our experience too shallow, our spiritual vision too dim to really grasp "the things which God hath prepared for them that love him" (1 Corinthians 2:9). But whether we can comprehend its glories or not, Jesus said, "When the Son of man shall come in his glory, and all the holy angels with him, then shall he sit upon the throne of his glory....Then shall the King say unto them on his right hand, Come, ye blessed of my Father, inherit the kingdom prepared for you from the foundation of the world" (Matthew 25:31, 34). Our entrance into heaven is not dependent upon our ability to comprehend its glories but upon our willingness to love its King while we are still residents of the earth.

Heaven will be large and lovely, filled with beauty and blessedness, and constructed of precious minerals and metal. But heaven is far more than the outer shell, the container.

CHAPTER 7

How Different Will the New Earth Be From the Old Earth?

TOURISTS MAY RESPOND to the antiquity of Rome, the excitement of Paris, or the historicity of Jerusalem, but even while they are visiting the city of their choice, they are aware, whether they see it or not, of another city within the city. For all of the beauty the tourist may be shown, there is also an area of poverty, prostitution, privation, and perversion lurking somewhere in each city's surroundings. Warnings are repeatedly issued against theft, muggings, and other crimes, and certain areas are declared "off limits" in the tourists' guides. Cities are a mixture of good and bad, of honesty and dishonesty. Beauty in one section is offset by the filth of another section. Palatial colleges are offset by paltry slums, while magnificent mansions are outweighed by the hundreds of homeless who sleep in the streets.

Even those cities that manage to curb some of these problems have lost control of pollution. More and more, the tourist must carry his own bottled water, and he finds fresh air totally unavailable. In many of our cities the sun cannot be seen in the city even when the sky is cloudless. Man seeks to build a lovely habitation, but he seldom succeeds more than halfway. Forces over which he has no control early defile his best efforts.

But this is not so in our heavenly Jerusalem. Having described the beauty of its walls, the gold of its streets, and the glistening crystal of its buildings, John begins to list the things that will forever be excluded from this city of God's design. In the concluding verses of Revelation 21, John enumerates seven specifics that will not be part of this heaven.

WILL WE WORSHIP GOD IN A TEMPLE?

Unlike the order in which we would make exclusions in trying to achieve the perfect city, John begins with the things we now see as the most desirable essentials and proceeds to the undesirable elements. The first exclusion is given in verse 22: "And I saw no temple therein: for the Lord God Almighty and the Lamb are the temple of it." No temple? But isn't worship what heaven is all about? Here on Earth we habitually equate a place of worship with worship itself. We have expended much energy and vast sums of money to construct temples of one kind or another throughout the world. Wars have been fought over them, and men have dedicated their entire lives to their preservation and maintenance. Pastors are sometimes jealous over their churches, and congregations have been known to become competitive over them. How can we conceive of heaven without a temple or a church structure?

When the Israelites were brought out of Egypt by the mighty hand of God, they were offered a personal relationship with God at Mount Sinai. He offered to make them a kingdom of priests (Exodus 19:6) with direct access to their God, but this proved to be too much for their faith to grasp, so God offered them a substitute, called a tabernacle.

In it He gave them rituals, rites, ceremonies, and sacrifices to help them in their approach to His holy presence in the holy of holies.[1] The priesthood, the prescribed offerings, the perfumed incense, and the public responses formed the basis of their worship. All of this was done outside the presence of God, in the outer court or in the holy place. But on the day of atonement when the high priest went into the special chamber reserved for God's presence, ritual gave way to reality. On this one day per year he was granted direct communication with God. He no longer needed the cloud of incense to symbolize the presence of God; he stood in the manifested presence of God called the *Shekinah* (cloud of God's glory). The high priest and God fellowshiped on a one-to-one basis in this perfect cube, lavishly ornamented with golden furniture and gold on three walls, with the fourth wall decorated of white linen embroidered with variegated colors. No other means were necessary.

When the saints get into God's greater cube, surrounded by gold and intricate colors, of which the tabernacle was only a miniature example, we will not need a temple with its rites and rituals. We too will fellowship with God on a one-to-one basis. There will be free and unhindered fellowship with God and His beloved Son, the Lamb. No particular place will be needed for the saints to assemble, for every place will be luminous with the divine presence and glory of God. As Vincent puts it, "The entire city is now one holy temple of God."[2]

The writer of the Book of Hebrews explains it, "But ye are come unto mount Sion, and unto the city of the living God, and heavenly Jerusalem, and to an innumerable company of angels, to the general assembly and *church of the firstborn*" (Hebrews 12:22–23, emphasis added). In heaven we don't have to "go to church"; we will *be* the church. There will be no difference between the sacred and the secular, for everything, including the inhabitants, will be God's and in harmony with Him. People living on level three won't have to worry about traveling up to level fifteen hundred to worship; all of heaven is God's temple, and every street or avenue will be as sacred as our most solemn cathedrals on this earth. The worship there will be immediate and direct, incessant and delightful.

God is going to come from behind all veils and make Himself available perpetually. We will no longer see Him "through a glass darkly; but then face to face" (1 Corinthians 13:12). The present infirmities of our flesh and the hindrances of our undeveloped spirits will all be done away with, and we will both stand and enjoy His presence without the intermediaries of ritual or ceremony. There we will learn that the only temple we need is Jesus, heaven's Lamb. When the disciples were walking with Jesus in the land of Palestine, they had a temple wherever He was—in the wilderness, in the boat, on the mountainside, or in the garden. They learned that where Jesus was, worship was possible. Similarly, the means of grace will cease when the end of grace comes, and church ordinances will give place to the God of ordinance. There will be no need for temples. The Lord will be temple enough.

When we get into the radiant New Jerusalem and discover that God has brought His throne into this city, His divine glory will make the entire city one continuous temple unto the Lord. We will hold direct communion with His manifest presence that fully encompasses all in all. As consecrated high priests we will then have come into the holiest of all places, the recognized presence of God.

WHAT WILL HAPPEN TO THE SUN AND MOON?

Furthermore, there will be no need for the sun or the moon. John states, "And the city had no need of the sun, neither the moon, to shine in it: for the glory of God did lighten it, and the Lamb is the light thereof" (Revelation 21:23). This, of course, seems strange to us earthlings who have come to recognize the sun as the source of all energy and life, directly or indirectly. We are indebted to the sun for the deposits of oil, gas, and coal in our earth, and we are just beginning to learn how dependent we are upon them. Also, all plant and animal life depend upon sunshine—no light, no life. If we lost our sun, the earth's orbit would lose its center pivot, our gravity would become disoriented, and life as we now know it would cease. In a thousand other ways we are dependent upon the sun and its counterbalance, the moon, just to sustain our lives. And yet John declares that in the New Jerusalem we will not need a sun or a moon.

Why? Because they will have been replaced with something greater. They are only created light, but our city will be illuminated by the presence of the Creator. Repeatedly the Bible has declared that "God is light, and in him is no darkness at all" (1 John 1:5). Part of God's essential nature is light—divine light. In the New Jerusalem, God will be the source of all radiant illumination. It will glisten with the colors of the rainbow while illuminating in shadow-free, nonglaring fashion. This light will not only illuminate; it will rejuvenate, for it will be life-giving.

Who will need a sun for energy when God, whose very voice created the world and everything that is in it, is radiating His iridescent glory? Who will need the stored-up energy of coal or oil when God's Son, who cleansed the lepers, opened blind eyes, and raised the dead with a single touch of

His hand, is in the midst of the city? Now we understand physical energy and natural power, but then we will begin to understand spiritual energy and divine power. Now we know how to convert energy from one form to another, but then we will see energy created in the form that is needed. Since there will never be any shortages, nothing will need to be stored up for future needs. Everything will function in God's eternal now.

Similarly, we will not need the gravitational pull of the sun and moon to maintain the earth's rotation, axis, or orbit. Everything will center around God; He will become the attraction around which the earth revolves. His presence will govern the action of the tides and the rotation of the earth. At that time we will better understand what Paul meant when he wrote, "For in him we live, and move, and have our being" (Acts 17:28). Everything will be subject to His authority and dominion: "[God] hath put all things under his [Christ's] feet, and gave him to be the head over all things to the church, which is his body, the fulness of him that filleth all in all" (Ephesians 1:22–23). Just as life in the old heavens and earth revolves around and is dependent upon the sun, so life in the new heavens and earth will rotate around and rely upon God.

Can there be life without the sun?

Of course, for the sun is merely God's agent for dispensing life to our present world. But God is not only defined as being "light"; He is also called "life." In our glorified bodies we will be able to receive life directly from His presence. No osmosis or photosynthesis will be necessary, for "in him was life; and the life was the light of men" (John 1:4). He who will become our light source will also become our life source. To walk in His light will be to walk in His life. The very radiance of His light will bring a rejuvenation of life within us. The eternal life that we now examine doctrinally we will then experience daily.

The Bible records a few instances of men who experienced this light. When Moses came down from Mount Sinai after forty days of communion with God, his face was so brilliantly radiant that the elders of Israel could not look on it; he had to wear a veil when in their presence. He had been in such close fellowship with that divine light that he became infused with it and entered Israel's camp as the lamp of God.

Similarly, when Paul was en route to Damascus, a light brighter than the sun at noontime shone round about him, irradiating his whole being with new sights and understanding and transforming his whole being into the light of the Lord. His heavenly commission was "to open their [Gentile's] eyes, and to turn them from darkness to light" (Acts 26:18). Even more outstanding was Christ's transfiguration when the light of God so streamed forth from the body and clothing of our Lord Jesus as to be terrifying to the disciples.

How glorious it will be when all of the saints live in the sunshine of God's living presence so that we too can radiate the blessed beauty of the light of God's presence!

But John does not limit this light to the inhabitants of the New Jerusalem. He declares, "And the nations of them which are saved shall walk in the light of it: and the kings of the earth do bring their glory and honour into it" (Revelation 21:24). Our heavenly city will become the source of both natural and spiritual illumination for the whole world. The light of truth and righteousness, and the light of life for *all* needs—personal, social, and national—shall shine forth from our eternal home to the nations that remain upon the earth. We glibly talk of Christian nations, but there has never truly been such a thing on the face of the earth. But when all darkness of sin shall forever be removed from creation and divine illumination of God's glory shines from the New Jerusalem upon this entire world, then nations shall be sanctified as holy. Then they will be Christian nations, for their life source, their illumination, and their center of interest will be God Himself. Then Christ will finally be seen as "the light *of the world*" (John 8:12, emphasis added).

In saying that "the kings of the earth do bring their glory and honour into it," John may be viewing Christ and His glorified saints, for Christ will have been crowned "King of kings and Lord of lords" (Revelation 19:16). We will have been made "kings and priests unto God" (Revelation 1:6; 5:10). All will reside in this heavenly city that will become the central seat of government for the whole world. But if by "kings *of the earth*" John refers to sub-kings belonging to unglorified humanity, he implies that the homage and gratitude of earthly royalty will devote everything of greatness and glory that it possesses to the service and honor of the New Jerusalem. All the honor the world can give will be given to that city. All eyes and all ears will be tuned to it, for it—and it alone—will be the source of life and light for the entire world. Only the glory of God's brightness that envelops this city like an unclouded halo and permeates and radiates through and from it so that there is not a dark or obscure place about it will illuminate the earth.

WILL THE CITY GATES BE PERPETUALLY OPENED OR CLOSED?

A third thing that John insists we will not see in heaven is a locked gate: "The gates of it shall not be shut at all by day" (Revelation 21:25). And, of course, there is no night, so the gates will be opened perpetually. Here in our earthly cities locked doors are normal, even required. Security is a prime necessity for the preservation of property and life. But in heaven the great angelic beings that stand guard alongside each of the twelve gates are sufficient security for all of heaven's inhabitants. There will be no closed doors to hinder our communication and communion with the inhabitants of the earth, nor need we ever fear that leaving the city for a time on Earth might jeopardize our return. We will never be barred from going out or coming in. Undoubtedly we will go out in service for the Lord and come back for worship unto the Lamb.

How often during our earthly pilgrimage have we accepted a commission for service while in the presence of God, only to discover that Satan had locked the doors of opportunity to us? Paul seemed to experience this on several occasions, and he asked the saints in Colossae to "continue in prayer...for us, that God would open unto us a door of utterance, to speak the mystery of Christ, for which I am also in bonds" (Colossians 4:2–3). Christ promised the church in Philadelphia, "I have set before thee an open door, and no man can shut it" (Revelation 3:8). When we get to heaven there will be no shut doors. Nothing can ever hinder service to the Master, and nothing can impede our entrance into the divine presence. There will never be a closed gate in heaven—only angelic guards to constantly assure us of our safety in the heavenly places.

The fourth thing John adds to further aid our sense of security is this: "There shall be no night there" (Revelation 21:25). There can be no darkness occasioned by the going down of the sun, for there is no sun or moon. Here on Earth, all daylight has been followed by darkness—even spiritually, all coming into His presence has been followed by going out from His presence. But in the New Jerusalem we will continually be in the light of His divine presence and surrounded by the glory of God, which will have become the light of the city. There will be no need for activities to stop because of nightfall or exhaustion; there will be no need of a period of daily rest for our bodies to recuperate, for our glorified bodies will function without the pause for sleep. No night, no darkness! John was so impressed with this that he repeated it in chapter 22, saying, "And there shall be no night there; and they need no candle, neither light of the sun; for the Lord God giveth them light" (verse 5). There will never be any form of substitute light: no candles, lamps, electric lights, or illuminated gases. Since there will be no darkness to cover evil deeds or to give occasion to lawlessness, we will not need artificial light; we will have a perpetual supply of the real thing.

HOW DO WE KNOW HEAVEN IS VOID OF SIN?

Seldom do we view a beautiful scene in this world without being aware of something that defiles it aesthetically. Sometimes a single dilapidated building stands out among surrounding, well-built structures, or it may merely be metal cans strewn across the landscape. Man usually defiles the aesthetic enjoyment of our world. But in heaven nothing will ever be out of place; the symmetry will never be broken, the colors will never clash, the cleanliness will never be dirtied, and the air will never be polluted. John exclaims, "And there shall in no wise enter into it any thing that defileth" (Revelation 21:27). What a relief! Heaven's parks will not need cleanup crews armed with bags and spiked poles, nor will heaven's city ever need garbage collectors, for nothing that defiles will ever enter into the city.

Although I am referring to mere aesthetics, of course this would also include ceremonial defilement. The priests in the Old Testament type of heaven, the tabernacle, had to repeatedly cleanse themselves ceremonially with sprinklings of blood and washings of water. They were prohibited from entering the holy place without stopping at the laver to wash their hands, faces, and feet. To do so was to risk immediate death (Exodus 30:20). Time after time, day after day, they had to go through purification rites before they dared enter the first court of God's presence. But in heaven we will not need ceremonial washings. As a matter of fact, heaven's laver is a sea of glass (Revelation 15:2); no water is available for ceremonial cleansings since there is nothing in heaven that can defile us. There will be no need for "foot washings" in heaven, and no need for a purifying of our minds, for there will be no impure motives, no evil thoughts, no fears, or no faithlessness. Nothing that could defile the purity that the blood of the Lamb produced will be allowed entrance to our holy residence. With Satan cast into the lake of fire and sin forever purged from the heavens and the earth, there will be no source of defilement. No matter how loving our relationships may be, there will never be anything that defiles us morally—never a questionable act, glance, word, or thought. All interpersonal relationships will be without defilement since there is nothing in the city that can defile us, morally or physically. The floors will not need to be swept, the furniture will never need dusting, the clothes will not need to be sent to the cleaners, and the dishes probably won't even have to be washed, because "there shall in no wise enter into it anything that defileth."

WILL THOSE WHO KILL IN THE NAME OF GOD ENTER HEAVEN?

In certain religions believers are taught that in order to enter into heaven, they must kill others in the name of their god. The Crusades from the eleventh to thirteenth centuries were fought in order to defeat Islam and win back the Holy Land. Many people on both sides fought, killed, and died in the "name of God."[3] But Revelation 21 makes it clear that everything that works abomination will be barred from heaven eternally (verse 27). As used in our English language, the word *abomination* refers to extreme disgust and hatred. In the New Testament it is used six times. In Matthew 24:15 it refers to "the abomination of desolation, spoken of by Daniel the prophet," which was religious murder that produced martyrs. Killing others "in the name of God" has always been a loathsome thing to God, whether it was killing the body, the man's spirit, or his reputation. Jesus used this word in responding to the derision of the Pharisees when He said, "Ye are they which justify yourselves before men; but God knoweth your hearts: for that which is highly esteemed among men is abomination in the sight of God" (Luke 16:15). Religious pride and self-seeking has always produced utter disgust on God's part. It occasioned the expulsion of Satan from heaven and is still the number one thing that separates man from God. Two times the word *abomination* is used in Revelation 17:4–5, where it speaks of religious impurity and filthiness. God has always intensely disliked sexual impurity done in the name of "love" or as a religious act. It is an abomination in His sight.

Make no mistake about it. Heaven will forever bar abomination. There will be no more killing for "the faith" or religious pride that causes men to exalt themselves above others; neither will there be any religious impurity done in the name of God. All response to God will be pure in its motivation and manifestation. There will be no mixture of impurity, no leaven of pride, and no putting down of another. At the gates the angels will stop anything that could in any wise work abomination.

HOW DO WE KNOW WE WON'T SIN?

If Lucifer, who was once a citizen of heaven, was capable of sinning, then how do we know we too are not susceptible to sinning when we get there?

As I said earlier, heaven will be void of sin. The seventh thing that John declares will not be admitted into heaven is "any thing…that maketh a lie" (Revelation 21:27). Here on Earth we have to constantly judge between truth and error— false and true. Even in the religious realm we have had to contend with deceit, exaggeration, extortion, fraud, and lies. But in heaven nothing that is deceitful will gain admittance. The Phillips version translates this verse, "Nothing unclean, no one who deals in filthiness and lies, shall ever at any time enter it."

How often have we have witnessed someone through whom we have received much spiritual truth become an instrument of deceit, through whom a lie comes that wounds, damages, and often destroys the work the truth had accomplished? When we get to heaven we will not have to constantly "try the spirits" (1 John 4:1); we will not have to "prove all things [and] hold fast that which is good" (1 Thessalonians 5:21). God the Father, God the Son, and God the Holy Spirit are totally incapable of lies, for part of God's essential nature is "I am the truth." How relaxing it will be to walk down street after street, mile after mile, knowing that everything we see, hear, and experience is the truth. Every scintillating sensation we will experience will be the truth. "Nothing that maketh a lie" will be there.

One of the joys the disciples found in walking with Jesus was that every word He ever spoke was the truth. They never had to take anything with "a grain of salt," or check on the facts after one of His teachings. Neither will we ever have to double-check anything in heaven; everything and everyone will be truthful. "All liars shall have their part in the lake which burneth with fire and brimstone" (Revelation 21:8); there is no place for liars in God's holy city. Heaven is a prepared place for a prepared people and is to be shared with a holy God. If during the millennial reign of Christ, holiness will be so predominant that "in that day shall there be upon the bells of the horses, HOLINESS UNTO THE LORD, and...every pot in Jerusalem and in Judah shall be holiness unto the LORD of hosts" (Zechariah 14:20–21), how much more shall *holiness* be the theme of heaven!

Rev. John Stoughton of England said many years ago, "Without holiness there can be no such heaven as the New Testament reveals. There may be scenery of surpassing grandeur—mountains, woods, rivers, and skies, most charming; but they do not make a heaven, else a heaven might be found in Wales or Cumberland. There may be a capital full of palaces and temples; but they do not make a heaven, else a heaven might have been found in Delhi. There may be buildings of marbles and precious stones; but they do not make a heaven, else a heaven might have been in Rome or Venice. There may be health, and ease, and luxury, festivities: but they do not make a heaven, else one would have been met with in Belshazzar's halls. There may be education, philosophy, poetry, literature, art; but that will not make a heaven, else the Greeks would have had one in Athens, in the grove and in the porch. Holiness is that without which no heaven could exist."[4]

But our heaven will have holiness, for holiness is an imperative, inflexible, eternal condition of heaven. It is called the "holy city" (Revelation 21:2); it is the home of a holy God; a holy Jesus will be there, surrounded by His holy angels (Matthew 25:31); the Holy Spirit will be in the throne room; and heaven's citizenship will be made up of holy people (Hebrews 3:1). What a marked contrast it will be to the life we have lived here on Earth! Our present residence is a God-cursed planet. We breathe an atmosphere in which Satan has his headquarters, we are surrounded by godless men, and we are repeatedly polluted by the ungodliness of the world system with which we do business. We have, since our conversion, groaned in our spirit, struggling to be freed from sin and to be wholly devoted to God, but in heaven the conflict will be over. That which our spirit has so longed for will be eternally enjoyed in our body, soul, and spirit: complete emancipation from sin and enslavement to God's most perfect and acceptable will. Holiness will forever be the inheritance of the saints. Nothing of an unholy nature will ever enter the sacred city to come against and pollute the saints. In that beautiful city "we shall be like him [Jesus]; for we shall see him as he is" (1 John 3:2).

DOES BEING A "GOOD PERSON" AUTOMATICALLY GRANT ME ENTRANCE INTO HEAVEN?

All men *might* go to heaven, but all men will not go to heaven. Only those men whose names have been written in the Lamb's Book of Life will ever be admitted. Sin separated us from fellowship with God (Romans 3:23), and consequently, we are not granted automatic access into His presence.

When we get to heaven, not only will we "be like him"; we shall be *with* Him. After John enumerates the seven things that will be excluded from the New Jerusalem, he says, "But they which are written in the Lamb's book of life [shall enter into it]" (Revelation 21:27). Heaven's citizenship is very definitely circumscribed. Men do not become citizens of heaven by entering the gates of the city; they are allowed entrance through the gates because they are already citizens. Advanced registration is a must!

Paul declares that "we are citizens of Heaven" (Philippians 3:20, PHILLIPS) and that we are "no longer aliens or foreign visitors; [we] are citizens like all the saints, and part of God's household" (Ephesians 2:19, JB). We do not belong here; we are "strangers and pilgrims on the earth" (Hebrews 11:13), and our present residence is spoken of as a heavenly embassy: "Now then we are ambassadors for Christ" (2 Corinthians 5:20). The world refuses to claim us as their own, but heaven declares that we belong to the kingdom of God. We have current citizenship status in both God's kingdom and His headquarters city, the New Jerusalem. We currently function as the personal representatives of God's divine government in an alien land—Earth.

When you receive Jesus Christ as Lord and Savior of your life, your name is written in the Lamb's Book of Life (Revelation 20:12). At your conversion you were assured that your name was duly recorded in heaven's Book of Life and given an "earnest of [your] inheritance"—the Holy Spirit (Ephesians 1:14)—as a pledge that the promise would be kept (sort of a down payment on the contract). The book in heaven and the Spirit in the earthly life of the believer are cross-references that safeguard the citizenship of heaven.

Each name in this book identifies one who has been purchased by and cleansed with the precious blood of the Lamb. Not only has each person received God's love, but they have also responded to it wholeheartedly. They have been willing to forsake the pursuit of earthly joys in preference to heaven's jubilation, for no possession on Earth seems enviable in comparison to the home that is made available to them in heaven. They prefer nomadic status here because their heavenly abode is so near, and they choose to lay up treasures in heaven rather than to amass fortunes on the earth. But theirs is no idle hope, no fanciful dream. They are responding to a promise.

Here on Earth the righteous and the wicked dwell together in the same country, the same city, and the same family; they are united by numerous relative, social, and civil ties. But in the future world they will be forever separated and will dwell in places as diverse and distant as heaven is from hell. Here the citizens of heaven have often been disdained and despised. The Scriptures say, "[They] had trials of cruel mockings, and scourgings, yea, moreover of bonds and imprisonment: they were stoned, they were sawn asunder, were tempted, were slain with the sword: they wandered about in sheepskins and goatskins; being destitute, afflicted, tormented; (of whom the world was not worthy:) they wandered in deserts, and in mountains, and in dens and caves of the earth" (Hebrews 11:36–38). Great is the grace of God that makes saints and citizens of heaven out of the earth's maligned and banished ones. It was the beggar Lazarus who was carried by the angels into Abraham's bosom, not the rich man; at Calvary, it was a thief condemned by earthly justice to the cross who was assured a place in paradise with the suffering Savior. How the false estimates, false reputations, false rewards of Earth are reversed and rectified in Christ's heaven!

Likewise, the divergent values of life will be forever separated, for heaven is not subjected to the financial and social influences of this world. Its society is not based on money or any of its tributaries, incidents, or accidents. Purity of character reigns in heaven, but money does not. About the time that all things earthly are dissolved and the treasures of the wicked are lost forever, the righteous will enter into heaven and take possession of durable riches and righteousness— treasures incorruptible, undefiled, and never to fade away.

Only the redeemed shall enter heaven, and they bring the principles of their Redeemer with them. They have lived by heaven's rules while separated from its reality; now they will love those laws, being secure in all of their benefits.

Are there restrictions in heaven?

In some aspects, heaven is a restricted city. For instance, it limits the emotional experiences that its citizens may experience. John declares, "And God shall wipe away all tears from their eyes; and there shall be no more death, neither sorrow, nor crying, neither shall there be any more pain: for the former things are passed away" (Revelation 21:4). Heaven will be a place of joy, and nothing that would limit that joy will be permitted.

After telling His disciples about His Father's house

and that they would abide in the Father's house, Jesus said, "These things have I spoken unto you, that my joy might remain in you, and that your joy might be full" (John 15:11). Fulfillment of joy and being filled with joy are the expected norm of heaven. As we enter the city, God will wipe away all tears from our eyes, and from that day on there will be no crying. No disappointments, no heartaches, no frustrations, no unfulfilled longings after God will ever stir our emotions to tears again. Laughter, love, songs, and shouts will be heard throughout eternity, but no crying will ever dampen the enjoyment of the New Jerusalem.

Also, there will be no physical or emotional pain. Never will the pain of remembered sins pierce our conscience, nor will the absence of one in heaven who was loved on Earth cause grieving or hurt. From the heavenly perspective we will see that God is just and that sufficient opportunity for repentance was offered that friend while he lived on Earth. Moreover, since we will be forever rid of our earthly body and eternally clothed with our immortal body, physical pain will be an impossibility. No disease, accident, or torture will be available to heaven's citizens. We will live immune to pain and to death, for "death is swallowed up in victory" (1 Corinthians 15:54).

Commenting on this passage, Edward M. Bounds said:

> But heaven's state will be one of supreme, unalloyed happiness, with nothing to shadow its brightness, nothing to bring pain, or cause sorrow. There is ineffable joy, no void, no fear, no anxiety, no alloy.
>
> "No sickness." What an immeasurable bliss! "No pain." What endless comfort and ease! "No sorrow," no cloud, no night, no weariness, no bitterness, no anguish, no penitence, no remorse, no graves, no sighs,

no tears, no sad laments, no broken hearts, no death-bed scenes, no dying there. Never a corpse, never a coffin, never a hearse, never a grave in all that happy, thrice-blissful land. No funeral crowd ever wept, nor sorrowing ones ever pass through its streets, or walk along its cloudless highways. Not only is there an absence of these things, which destroy earth's brightest bliss. Their absence is enough to form a delightful heaven.[5]

Everything that would hinder our enjoyment of life will be prohibited in heaven, for the New Jerusalem is more than a limited city; it is a living city. And we will fully enjoy its varied expressions of that life.

CHAPTER 8

What Will Life in Heaven Be Like?

AN INFANT ENTERS life in this world in total helplessness and often leaves this earthly realm as an adult amid the helplessness of infirmity. But between its coming and going, life is a blessed, divine gift entrusted to mankind by a beneficent God. What a man makes of that life is often more the result of chance and circumstance than diligent determination, but whether that life is lived in opulence or poverty, it is guarded as the most priceless gift ever to be received. Without it nothing else matters. Kings have offered their kingdoms for a guaranteed extension of merely one more year of life, and the wealthy have spent fortunes trying to find the secret of perpetual youth.

It is inherent in the nature of man to desire to live perpetually, for man was made in the image and likeness of God, who is eternal in His nature. When Jesus was on this earth, one of His favorite topics was eternal life. Throughout the Gospel of John, Christ spoke of Himself as being the source of life, applying at least seven different metaphors:

1. The *water* of life (John 4:14)
2. *Inherent* life (John 1:4; 5:26)
3. The *bread* of life (John 6:48)
4. The *blood* of life (John 6:53–54)

5. The *giver* of life (John 6:33)
6. The *word* of life (John 6:63, 69)
7. The *resurrection* of life (John 11:25)

The impartation of this eternal life was the purpose of the incarnation, crucifixion, resurrection, and ascension of Jesus, who declared, "I am come that they might have life, and that they might have it more abundantly" (John 10:10).

It is to be expected, then, that the final book of the Bible, which speaks so loudly of the culmination of all things, would also speak of life utilizing at least seven separate metaphors:

1. The *crown* of life (Revelation 2:10)
2. The *tree* of life (Revelation 2:7; 22:2, 14)
3. The *Book* of Life (Revelation 3:5; and six other times)
4. The *Spirit* of life (Revelation 11:11)
5. The *fountain of water of life* (Revelation 21:6)
6. The *river* of life (Revelation 22:1)
7. The *water* of life (Revelation 22:17)

It is not mere coincidence that the final three analogies are water, for water is essential to life as we know it in this realm. No form of life can exist without water, so when John moves from describing the exterior of the city in Revelation 21 to sharing what he could see of the interior of the city in Revelation 22, the first thing he describes is the living water.

The New Jerusalem is far more than beautiful foundation stones, pure golden streets, and crystal dwellings. All of this merely houses the people who make up the true city, for the character of any city is determined more by the people who inhabit it than by the physical structures that form the skyline. A city without citizens would be nothing more than an architectural showpiece or an expensive exhibition of building materials and skills. Since the psalmist tells us that "the heavens declare the glory of God; and the firmament sheweth his handywork" (Psalm 19:1), the New Jerusalem is not a showpiece of God's skill but is a dwelling place for His many sons. It is a city that is alive and active. Everything in it is full of life, and ample provision has been made to sustain that life perpetually.

But this life is not new, nor merely continuing; it is life fully consummated. It, like all of human history, had its beginnings in the Garden of Eden, and it is brought to completeness in the New Jerusalem. Genesis is the Book of Beginnings; the Revelation is the Book of the Endings of what was then begun, for the end of our redemption is both consistent with and a completion of the glimpses of the beginnings. Genesis and the history of mankind start with a paradise; Revelation ends with a paradise. Genesis begins with God imparting life to mankind, while Revelation ends with God providing eternal life for mankind.

It is interesting to see that what God established at the beginning of man's history comes full circle back to the beginning, welded into a perfect ring of eternity by His love. Man had his origins in that which was perfectly constructed of God for man, and he enters into eternity in that which is perfectly constructed of God for man—paradise. Man began in a time of innocence, which was followed by a long, dreary time of the absence of that innocence. Now in the last chapter of Revelation, John tells us that man ends back in a glorious period of innocence where there is no curse, no sin, no devil, and no defilement. How accurately Paul wrote, "Looking unto Jesus the author and finisher of our faith"

(Hebrews 12:2), and, "He which hath begun a good work in you will perform it until the day of Jesus Christ" (Philippians 1:6). In the context of this verse, the word *perform* in the Greek is *epiteleo*, which means, "to fulfill further or completely." All of God's beginnings have predetermined endings, and nothing that sin or Satan attempts will frustrate those plans. Man, made in God's image and for God's pleasure, will yet be brought back into that image, endowed with God's life, and returned to God's presence to again become the object of God's pleasure, "for the LORD taketh pleasure in his people" (Psalm 149:4).

LIFE TO ITS FULLEST

But heaven's paradise, river of life, and tree of life resemble those in Adam's Eden like a vegetable resembles the seed from which it came. All of the carrot is in the tiny seed, but it germinates, grows, matures, and ripens into a much more useful form than the seed that went into the earth. Similarly, the life seen in heaven is a maturation of the life revealed in Eden. It is the embryo brought to perfection. As E. M. Bounds phrases it, "The state, environments and advances of the heavenly world are all life, more life, deeper, wider, sweeter life."[1]

From his hilltop perspective, John could see into the city far enough to be aware of five manifestations of this ripened life. He describes a living river, a living tree, a living atmosphere, a living administration, and heaven's living service. Each seems to be the finished product of the limited workings of the Holy Spirit here on Earth.

The first speaks of the "rivers of living water" that Jesus said would flow out of the believing Christian (John 7:37–39), while the living tree speaks of the limited "fruit of the

Spirit" that these believers would manifest in their lives (Galatians 5:22–23). The atmosphere reminds us of the wind of the Spirit that Jesus discussed with Nicodemus (John 3:8) and that accompanied the first outpouring of the Spirit upon the infant church in Jerusalem (Acts 2:2). The living administration is the matured guidance that the Spirit has given to believers here on Earth (John 16:13). Obviously, the living service of heaven is but a ripening of the works and giftings of the Holy Spirit through believers during the period called "time" (1 Corinthians 12:4–11). If these manifestations have been glorious here on Earth, try to imagine their unrestricted operations in a sinless, fleshless setting. When God does not have to accommodate our exaggerated fears of the unknown, our limited faith in His promises, and our appalling ignorance of His Word and ways, what glories will be revealed! Heaven will have no limitations, for there "we shall see him as he is" (1 John 3:2).

Characteristics of the Afterlife

Some of the most beautiful sights on this earth are man-made memorials for the dead: auditoriums, mausoleums, tombs, memorial parks, and so forth. But the New Jerusalem is not a living *memorial*—it is a living *city*. Its water is the river of life; its trees are the tree of life. Even its atmosphere is alive. Heaven is not plagued with smog. Its buildings will never be stained with soot, and its language will never be defiled with smut. The air we breathe will be the purest imaginable, and its temperature will always be pleasant.

Those who have reported their visions of this New Jerusalem say that the atmosphere radiates with iridescent colors somewhat like the northern lights. They speak of the pleasant sensations they experienced just from the feel of this atmosphere on their bodies. Some have described it as being filled with the most beautiful music that a trained musician could ever conceive. Several of them have ended their descriptions by saying that this atmosphere gives an impression of being alive.

While those who have had visions of what life in heaven is like, all would probably agree that no description comes close to truly describing heaven. I believe, however, that the Scriptures give us a glimpse into at least five basic characteristics of what life is like in heaven:

1. It is a place where God dwells.
2. It is a place where the righteous dwell with God.
3. It is a place of great beauty.
4. It is a place of inestimable value.
5. It is a place of God's rule.

The fifth one we will cover in detail in the next chapter.

Where God dwells

Heaven is, indeed, a place where God dwells, but without taking away anything from the "Father's house" concept of heaven, we must admit that the Scriptures teach the omnipresence of God. God is now everywhere present, and the psalmist tells us that God inhabits the praises of His people (Psalm 22:3). Furthermore, Paul quotes from the Pentateuch when he writes, "God hath said, I will dwell in them, and walk in them; and I will be their God, and they shall be my people" (2 Corinthians 6:16; Leviticus 26:12). He further assures us that Christ and the Holy Spirit also dwell within us (Romans 8:9, 11; Ephesians 3:17). To whatever extent the concept of God in and among His people may become real to us, we will experience the beginnings of heaven here on Earth. Immanuel—God with us—is the beginning concept of heaven, and this commences at our first meeting with Christ at Calvary.

Where the righteous dwell with God

Heaven is also a place where the righteous dwell with a holy God. Every concept of God dwelling among His people also carries the transposed emphasis that His people are living in the presence of this holy God. "God with us," "God in us," and "God among us" all speak of our being in His presence. David declared:

> Lord, who shall abide in thy tabernacle? who shall dwell in thy holy hill? He that walketh uprightly, and worketh righteousness, and speaketh the truth in his heart.
>
> —Psalm 15:1–2

John reiterated this concept:

> And I heard a great voice out of heaven saying, Behold, the tabernacle of God is with men, and he will dwell with them, and they shall be his people, and God himself shall be with them, and be their God.
>
> —Revelation 21:3

We need to remind ourselves that the righteousness required in order to dwell in the presence of a holy God is not produced by death but is conferred to us by the life of Christ. It is the fact that we have embraced Jesus Christ as Savior and have received His righteousness that has made us fit for heaven, not the fact that we have expired and have received a proper burial.

It is both possible and imperative that we be as fit for heaven right now as at the moment of death, for death does not change us morally—only physically. We will either live righteously or die in our unrighteousness. If we reject Christ's righteousness and live in self-righteousness, whether morally good or bad, death will not bring us into God's presence; instead, it will forever separate us from that presence. But if we live righteously, we can enjoy the abiding presence of God right here on the earth. So at least the heavenly distinction of dwelling with God has its beginnings in the here and now.

A place of unsurpassed beauty

We have also presented heaven as a place of unsurpassed beauty, but even this has at least embryonic beginnings here in the church age, for the psalmist declares, "He will beautify the meek with salvation" (Psalm 149:4), and, "Let the beauty of the LORD our God be upon us" (Psalm 90:17). The prophets proclaimed, "The Spirit of the LORD God is upon me [Christ]...to give unto them beauty for ashes" (Isaiah 61:1, 3), and, "His beauty shall be as the olive tree" (Hosea 14:6). While the beauty of heaven's crystal city cannot be viewed now, the beauty of the Lord of glory is now being conferred to the future inhabitants. The Holy Spirit is presently at work within the true church, transforming us into the image of Christ, for Christ is going to "present it to himself a glorious church, not having spot, or wrinkle, or any such thing; but that it should be holy and without blemish" (Ephesians 5:27). God may begin with some very raw material, but He ends with beautiful jewels (Malachi 3:17). So to whatever extent we are allowing the beauty of Christ to replace the marks and stains of sin, we are already enjoying a small portion of heaven on the earth.

A place of incalculable value

For another thing, we have pictured heaven as a place of incalculable value. Peter says, "That the trial of your faith, being much more precious than of gold" (1 Peter 1:7), so it seems that in God's estimation some things are more valuable than gold, crystal, and gigantic gemstones. Peter uses this word *precious* seven of the ten times it appears in the New Testament. It is the Greek word *time*, a derivative of Peter's usage of *precious*, which means "esteem (especially of the highest degree)." Twice Peter speaks of our faith being precious (1 Peter 1:7; 2 Peter 1:1), and then he speaks of the precious chief cornerstone of that faith, Jesus Christ (1 Peter 2:6), the precious blood (1 Peter 1:19), the precious promises (2 Peter 1:4), and the fact that Christ, as a person, is precious (1 Peter 2:7). Just as Abraham's servant gave valuable gifts to Rebekah as an inducement for her to return with him to become Isaac's bride (Genesis 24:53), so the Holy Spirit has lavishly gifted the church with heaven's most valuable treasures to induce her to become Christ's bride. Embellished with divine faith and promises, beautified with the cleansing power of Christ's blood, and animated by His presence, the church has already entered into that which heaven calls valuable.

As the body of Christ we get a little foretaste of this living atmosphere in the wind, or breath, of the Holy Spirit as it was evidenced on the Day of Pentecost when we come together for worship. Occasionally we soar into high and holy worship levels, experiencing a tremendous sense of the Holy

Spirit's presence. But the truth is that even at our highest spiritual level, our spiritual life is smog-filled. As long as our spirits are housed in corruptible bodies, memories of evil are still active and the pain of sin has not yet been abated; our souls are smog-filled, spiritually speaking.

We never truly come into a total purity of heart and mind, for there is always something that taints and defiles. But the tiny breath of the Spirit that we enjoy here on Earth is only an "earnest of our inheritance." It is just enough to give us a foretaste for more. Although it is limited, it is vastly superior to anything else we experience in our spirit or soul level, and it gives us a tiny sample of what heaven's living spiritual atmosphere will really be like. John sums it up by simply saying, "And there shall be no more curse" (Revelation 22:3). This is because there is no sin, no desire to sin, no ability to sin, and no penalty because of sin. Heaven will be as sinless as Eden was before the Fall.

Could Satan tempt mankind again in the new earth?

You may say, "But man did fall. Although Adam was created specifically for this beautiful and glorious Eden over six thousand years ago, Satan entered the garden in the form of a serpent and enticed man into rebellion against the commandments of God. Couldn't the same thing happen in the new paradise of God?"

Thank God that by the time we get to the New Jerusalem, this Lucifer, as he was known in heaven, will be restricted forever to the lake that burns with fire and brimstone. He will no longer be the tempter of mankind or the accuser of the brethren.

"But," you might reason, "what about the other two

named angels who seem to be of the same rank as Lucifer? Is it possible that one of them could also rebel and in so doing drag us into his rebellion as Lucifer did to Adam?"

If we had to face this insecurity throughout eternity, much of heaven's joys would be forfeited, so God graciously assures us that there will be "no more curse." Nothing will transpire in heaven to separate us from the tree of life or the presence of God. The disappearance of sin will be an everlasting disappearance! The glory and blessedness of God's provision will never again give place to darkness, sin, and death. There will be no more sin. We can't get involved in something that is nonexistent.

And even more blessed than this is that there will be no desire to sin. Not only will we be unable to trip and fall in the mud of sin, but we won't even be looking for the mud to play in. There will be nothing within us that desires or craves for sin. It is not that man's volitional freedom will be taken away from him the moment he steps through the pearly gates into the city, for we have no reason to believe that man's will is going to be restrained in heaven any more than it was restrained in the garden. But the absence of a tempter, coupled with the training and experience that the redeemed will have undergone on Earth, will stand like a wall between them and anything that could tempt them to say, "My will, not Thine, be done."

Furthermore, our love for God and the depth of appreciation for our redemption, especially after we see the tremendous price Christ Jesus paid for its purchase, will be so great that no saint would submit to anything that would take it away from him. Besides, here on Earth we have learned that love is the greatest deterrent to the violation of law. How much more powerful this will be when we have entered into God's perfect love.

Moreover, we will have no ability to sin in the New Jerusalem. Joseph A. Seiss comments:

> Holy angels stand fast in their blessedness forever, not because they are less free to sin than were those who kept not their first estate; but because, having stood the test, the whole momentum of their moral being moves only towards what is true and good, and so they never fall.[2]

Such will be the security of the redeemed saints in glory. Sin distorted this world, but God will bring us through a process of purification, training, learning, and development.

Having learned to walk by faith and love in a victory won through great pain and suffering, we will have no more fuel left in us with which sin could kindle a fire. Just as once the refiner's fire has removed all of the dross from the silver (Proverbs 25:4), so it will be that when the heavenly refiner has melted us with increasing levels of heat through trials, failures, temptations, battles, pain, and suffering, there will come a time of total purity. Such purity will be greatly aided by our passing through the river of life, when there is nothing negative within us that the fire can release. You can get only so much dross out of silver, and then it is pure; and you can get only so much sin out of a redeemed man, and then he too is as pure as a newborn babe.

Jesus was able to say to His disciples, "The prince of this world cometh, and hath nothing in me" (John 14:30). How we all have longed to say the same thing here on Earth, and yet it seldom has the ring of authenticity. But once we joyfully pass through the river of life, there will be nothing left within us that is capable of responding to anything that is short of the perfect will of God.

In Eden, Adam ate of the tree of the knowledge of good and evil, but merely learned to know *evil*. Ever since then man has been tasting and experiencing the bitterness of this evil. But through Christ's redemption the saints will come to know *good*, and their hearts will never be turned from it. Sin's perversion will have no attraction once grace's provision has been fully manifested. If through mere knowledge of evil man's heart was turned to perform evil, how much more will man's heart be fixed to do good when he is finally made to know and experience good? But it will be a "good" not as it is defined on this earth—the absence of evil—but as it is revealed in heaven—the absolute nature of God. "The Lord *is* good" (Psalm 100:5, emphasis added).

Along with this is the realization that when man is finally and permanently redeemed, everything that has been disordered, disabled, or cursed for man's sake will also be permanently delivered (Romans 8:9–23). There will be no more penalty because of sin, for the removal of sin also removes the need for a penalty. "No more curse," John says.

God pronounced this judgment-curse after Adam and Eve chose to listen to the voice of the tempter rather than obey the voice of God.

> *Unto the woman* he said, I will greatly multiply thy sorrow and thy conception: in sorrow thou shalt bring forth children; and thy desire shall be to thy husband, and he shall rule over thee. And *unto Adam* he said, Because thou hast hearkened unto the voice of thy wife, and hast eaten of the tree, of which I commanded thee, saying, Thou shalt not eat of it: cursed is the ground for thy sake; in sorrow shalt thou eat of it all the days of thy life; thorns also and thistles shall it bring forth

> to thee; and thou shalt eat the herb of the field; in the
> sweat of thy face shalt thou eat bread, till thou return
> unto the ground; for out of it wast thou taken: for dust
> thou art, and unto dust shalt thou return.
>
> —GENESIS 3:16–19, emphasis added

The curse was placed upon woman, man, the earth, and the economy of things on the earth. It involves all the elements that man touches and everything that surrounds him. It affects what he eats and drinks, the air he breathes, the ground upon which he walks, and all growth of nature, including the conditions of the seasons and the sea. It has opened the avenues of disease, calamity, and death until the earth is no longer habitable for man beyond a few brief years. Everything negative in our life is negative because of the curse God put on this earth when man sinned. Everywhere and upon everything is flashed back to us the reality that there is a fearful condemnation hanging over men—that a curse of sin is festering in all that pertains to man and his dwelling place.

But thanks be to God, that curse is not incurable. The remedy has been provided in Christ Jesus through His achievement as the second Adam. He destroyed the works of the devil, put away sin forever, and restored all things back to God the Father. While this remedy may seem to be long in taking effect, that effect will be eternal. John heard the cry from the throne, "Behold, I make all things new" (Revelation 21:5). The effect of that renewal is the cessation of the curse—not on the holy city, for there never was a curse on it, but on the places where the curse had been placed: upon woman, man, the earth, and the economy of things on the earth. What a glorious, living atmosphere in which to "live, and move, and have our being" (Acts 17:28).

When we dwell in the living atmosphere of the New Jerusalem, we will never be reminded of the curse, either in the city itself or in our excursions down to the earth. We will enjoy the fulfillment of Christ's petition while He was here on the earth when He prayed that it should be "on earth, as it is in heaven" (Matthew 6:10). The living creatures, the angels, the elders, the bride, the redeemed saints, and all mankind on the earth will be locked into the perfect will of God forever, for the throne in the midst of the living city will become the seat of the living administration of heaven.

CHAPTER 9

Will We Rule on the New Earth?

F THERE IS one thing that history should have taught us by now, it is that it doesn't matter how well you build the city, how good its water or food supply may be, or how fine its atmosphere. If there is not a proper governing of the inhabitants, the city can soon become a veritable hell. Men cannot live in the close proximity the city fosters upon them without fixed rules and someone who is empowered to enforce those laws. The frontier towns of our Old West amply illustrated this. Until law was administered, every man did that which was right in his own eyes—just as in the Book of Judges— and chaos resulted. When a capable administrator came on the scene—a judge in Bible days and a lawman in the West— peace reigned, and society functioned harmoniously.

Yes, it takes more than facilities to make a livable city. For some years now Americans have spent many millions of dollars to tear out slum sections of cities and replace them with quality housing. But often, instead of the new facilities transforming the citizens, the inhabitants destroyed the buildings, so that within a very short time the new looked as bad as the old. Change in the inhabitants should have preceded, or at least accompanied, the change in the environment, but somehow we usually seem to lack the administration to produce such change.

But this will not be so in the New Jerusalem, for it will possess the finest living administration that has ever ruled in the affairs of men. John sums it up so simply when he says, "The throne of God and of the Lamb shall be in it" (Revelation 22:3). The throne is a symbol of royal authority, dominion, power, and rule, and throughout the Scriptures it is frequently associated with God, who is pictured as sitting on His throne surrounded by the heavenly host. He is described as administering righteous judgment from His throne and intervening in the affairs of men, even to the appointing or overthrowing of kings of the earth. His power and authority are absolute, and, as Lucifer learned, He tolerates no insurrection or insubordination. Although some may see His rule as totalitarian and dictatorial, the Scriptures never picture God as some despot, reveling in power. His throne is called "the throne of grace" (Hebrews 4:16), and His reign is called a righteous reign (Psalm 9:4). As the creator, He certainly should best understand how His creatures should function and relate one to another and to their God, and where He rules, harmony reigns.

So when John saw God's throne in the New Jerusalem, he saw the ultimate in government being made available to heaven's citizens. It is a monarchy—God in total authority. God will sit as King in heaven, for heaven's affairs will be administered not through democracy but through theocracy. God, not man, will rule.

But, of course, this is not the first time we have seen a throne in the Book of Revelation. There are progressive thrones in this revelation of Christ Jesus, just as we have seen progressive rule throughout the Old Testament. In the first three chapters of Revelation, Christ appears walking amid the golden lamp stands, observing and communicating with the seven churches of Asia. At this point no throne is visible, for the church was the only kingdom in the process of formation, and God does not choose to rule His church from a throne. He is ruling from the lamp stands; He is ruling by way of His Spirit in the midst of the church. He is ruling by walking in an intimate relationship with His church very much as He governed Israel during the years of her wilderness wanderings. She was led by God's cloud and governed by His voice just as the church is now led by God's Spirit and His Word. Both Israel and the church had a "mercy seat" or "throne of grace" to appeal to, but it was not seen as the seat of God's government.

The moment the attention of this book is turned from the church to the world, a throne appears with surroundings that indicate a very special dispensation for the old earth—a dispensation partly retributive and partly remedial. It is the throne of judgment that is used during the "day of the Lord," from which Christ enforces the principles of His kingdom by visitations of successive judgments upon the world. It is an antitype of the reign of the judges when the kingdom was not yet established. Later, after the rejoicing over the fall and destruction of Babylon, this throne disappears, and we see only the thrones of the "shepherding" saints, who for a time rule the nations with a rod of iron. It seems to answer to the days when David forced nations to submit to his will. After the last great rebellion of Satan, typified by Absalom's rebellion against his father, has been put down, we see the "great white throne." It is the final judgment throne with no signs of blessing or rewards, for it consigns the unholy and unrighteous dead into the lake of fire that burns eternally. Only then is the holy city brought down to take its position as the final throne of God and the Lamb, who will govern the affairs of heaven, the earth, and all of their inhabitants.

This throne, seen in the New Jerusalem, is a throne not of judgment but of government. It is concerned not with punishment but with peace. Righteousness rather than justice is its office, and its purpose is to rule more than to reward. It is the final throne of God—His eternal throne— and from this throne He will reign in righteousness and justice. We will be free forever from deceitful politics, false religion, or oppressive tyranny. God will act justly and kindly and defend His glory as He manifests His holiness and His grace in ways far greater than we have ever known during the church age. Everything administered from this throne will be life, for there is no more death once the New Jerusalem is made operable.

For the many millions of people who lived in great political bondage on the earth, never knowing a single day of true freedom, this reign of Christ's righteousness will be all glorious, and the martyrs who suffered such religious intolerance will be content under God's administration. Even those who have known religious freedom and political security will rejoice at the vast superiority of Christ's way of governing.

Perhaps Psalm 47 will be our theme song on the day the throne becomes operative:

> Come, everyone, and clap for joy! Shout triumphant praises to the Lord! For the Lord, the God above all gods, is awesome beyond words; he is the great King of all the earth. He subdues the nations before us, and will personally select his choicest blessings for his Jewish people—the very best for those he loves.
>
> God has ascended with a mighty shout, with trumpets blaring. Sing out your praises to our God, our King. Yes, sing your highest praises to our King, the

King of all the earth. Sing thoughtful praises! He reigns above the nations, sitting on his holy throne. The Gentile rulers of the world have joined with us in praising him—praising the God of Abraham—for the battle shields of all the armies of the world are his trophies He is highly honored everywhere.

—PSALM 47:1–9, TLB

One charge that the world and some religionists have levied against the doctrine of heaven is that it is unrealistic, ethereal. They have mockingly stated that futuristic Christians are "so heavenly minded they are no earthly good." They add, "Give me something for the here and now, and I'll take my chances on the hereafter."

But neither our hope of heaven nor its reality is totally in the future.

A PLACE WHERE GOD RULES

In the previous chapter I listed four basic characteristics of life in heaven. But it is the fifth characteristic of heaven that is the most evident "earnest of our inheritance" (Ephesians 1:14). Heaven is a place of God's rule and God's dominion. Heaven is a kingdom. It has a King, a throne, and an administration of attendants and servants who will administer the will of God throughout the ends of the earth. "Thy will be done, on earth as it is in heaven" will become the norm. The psalmist declared, "All nations whom thou hast made shall come and worship before thee, O Lord; and shall glorify thy name" (Psalm 86:9).

But God's kingdom is not future; it exists right now. This is now our Father's world, not Satan's (Psalm 24:1–2); Jesus Christ is now "Lord of lords, and King of kings" (Revelation

17:14); and Jesus said, "All authority in heaven and on earth has been given to me" (Matthew 28:18, RSV). Nonetheless, God is not exerting His authority and position in the world today; He is allowing man the opportunity to learn the impossibility of self-rule, while also granting Satan an extended period of control in the governmental affairs of nations.

At present God has merely set boundaries beyond which neither man nor devil may go, and He is confining His personal rule and authority to heaven and His church. It is among His saints that He now reigns in life. His word is law and order for the believer, and the Holy Spirit enforces God's will—He convinces "the [church] world concerning sin and righteousness and judgment" (John 16:8, RSV), and takes the things of Christ and makes them real to Christians (John 16:14).

God rules His church from the midst of the candlesticks and shares His word and will through His written Word and His chosen servants (Ephesians 4:11–12). Obedience is optional, for there is no coercion, but divine blessings are shared with the obedient ones and are withheld from the self-ruled ones.

Jesus taught the availability of God's kingdom to men here on the earth in the period called time. "Seek ye first the kingdom of God and his righteousness," He said, "and all these things shall be added unto you" (Matthew 6:33). He recognized the coexistence of two kingdoms: God's and man's; the spiritual and the natural; righteousness and things.

All of us now live where two existing world systems share the same planet, the same span of time, and the same population. We are involved in both kingdoms. As people we must work, eat, sleep, and so forth, but as Christians we seek a relationship with the higher spiritual kingdom. At present we cannot divorce ourselves completely from the earthly realm, but we can refuse to let it have the rule of our lives. Paul reminded us in the Book of Romans that "the kingdom of God is not meat and drink; but righteousness, and peace, and joy in the Holy Ghost" (Romans 14:17). He, like Jesus, did not deny the demands of the flesh; he merely stated that they did not comprise God's kingdom. Jesus said the "things" of the world kingdom would be added as needed to the person who has set the attaining of God's kingdom as his highest goal.

In directing us to seek God's kingdom, Jesus was surely establishing that there is now an entrance to that kingdom; else why the injunction to seek it? If seeking God's kingdom of righteousness is to be our highest goal and the primary drive of our life, then it must be attainable, because Jesus never set the unattainable before anyone. "Ask, and it shall be given you; seek, and ye shall find; knock, and it shall be opened unto you," Jesus promised in Luke 11:9.

Furthermore, Christ said, "The kingdom of God is come upon you" (Luke 11:20), and "The kingdom of God is within you" (Luke 17:21). God's kingdom is not a billion light-years away; it is here, on us, in us! It is just that our spiritual eyes are dim—we cannot see God's kingdom for seeing the natural kingdom around us. But whether or not we can see it, it exists here and now.

If your dog could talk, he would argue that there are no colors in the world because he cannot see them. He would insist that everything in the world is black and white.

"You silly dog," you might say, "anyone in his right mind can see that there are reds, greens, blues, yellows, and many shades of color in between."

"But I'm in my right mind," he might answer, "and I can't see them."

So it is with many of us. We cannot see God's righteous kingdom, His angelic hosts, or the authority of His throne in the world today, so we do not believe that it exists. However, we need to cry, "Open my eyes that I might see."

Jesus told Nicodemus, "Except a man be born again, he cannot see the kingdom of God" (John 3:3), which implies that subsequent to the new birth experience comes a spiritual seeing. Much as the infant has to learn to discern what he is seeing, the recent convert does not understand all that he perceives, but at least he has an awareness of God's world all around him. He sees shapes, colors, and movements that convince him of reality, whether he can immediately translate that into applicable knowledge or not. At least he can now see; he has an inner awareness that God's kingdom is real.

Jesus said that the kingdom was here, was now, was upon us, and was within us. Furthermore, He said that we should be seeking to enter it, for God offers an advance entrance to His kingdom to those who will seek it. He offers us a little bit of heaven to go to heaven in, for heaven is not all future; it has its beginnings in our hearts. We are not merely looking for something in the sweet by-and-by; it is possible to enjoy something heavenly in the nasty here and now.

THE BEST IS YET TO COME!

But although through Christ's redemption we can be set free from sin's power, pollution, penalty, presence, and guilt, thereby making it possible to enter into God's kingdom of love and grace, all of this is but a very tiny portion of the fullness we will enjoy in heaven.

When Jesus turned the water into wine at Cana of Galilee, the governor of the feast, after sampling this miracle wine, called the bridegroom and said, "Every man at the beginning doth set forth good wine; and when men have well drunk, then that which is worse: but thou hast kept the good wine until now" (John 2:10). The best wine was last. Couple this with Christ's statement at the Last Supper: "I will not drink henceforth of this fruit of the vine, until that day when I drink it new with you in my Father's kingdom" (Matthew 26:29). Having supped of the cup, He said that the next time they shared eating and drinking together would be in heaven at the marriage supper of the Lamb (Revelation 19:9) and that it would be "new."

The best wine will be last. The friendship, fellowship, and feasting that we have enjoyed here with Christ and His church will be so superseded by heaven's family relationships as to cause us to forget the earthly joys of being a Christian. Earth's joy at forgiveness of sins will be overshadowed by heaven's sinlessness, and Earth's special gifts of grace that blessed, comforted, and healed us will dim into oblivion in the brightness of God's continual grace and glory that will be constantly available to us.

The best is yet to come! "Eye hath not seen, nor ear heard, neither have entered into the heart of man, the things which God hath prepared for them that love him. But God hath revealed them unto us by his Spirit" (1 Corinthians 2:9–10). This limited revelation is enough to excite the overcoming Christian to renewed faith and hope, for better days are ahead for all of us.

After quoting Christ as promising, "Behold, I come quickly; and my reward is with me, to give every man according as his work shall be" (Revelation 22:12), John adds,

"Blessed are they that do his commandments, that they may have right to the tree of life, and may enter in through the gates into the city" (verse 14).

Blessed, indeed! Eternally blessed! Heaven's happy home will be their heritage, sons of the most high God will be their parentage, and fellowship with Christ will be their privilege. "Even so, come, Lord Jesus" (Revelation 22:20)!

CHAPTER 10

What Will My Body Look Like?

PERHAPS WE NEED to remind ourselves that we are not mere spirits; we are spirit, soul, and body. We live in a body, and the Word teaches us that we will always live in a body. We will never get rid of our body; we will merely be allowed to exchange this mortal flesh for an immortal being. This terrestrial body will become celestial, but we will be spirit, soul, and body throughout all of eternity. Paul clearly declares that "there is a natural body, and there is a spiritual body" (1 Corinthians 15:44) and teaches us that Jesus, who was the last Adam and the second man (1 Corinthians 15:45, 47), ascended into heaven with a glorified body of the same type we shall have throughout all eternity and that He will return to this earth in that bodily form. Paul also says, "Just as each of us now has a body like Adam's, so we shall some day have a body like Christ's" (1 Corinthians 15:49, TLB).

Since this is so, a purely spiritual heaven could never accommodate people who will always have bodies. If we are always going to be substance, we will need a heaven that has substance. God's Word teaches us that there is a literal, honest-to-goodness, solid, substantial heaven that is just as real as, although different from, this literal, solid-substance earth we live on.

To some Christians this is a violation of their spiritual concepts and vision. But we need to learn the difference between a paradise of sense and a paradise of sensuality. Heaven is so real that our senses can perceive it, but that doesn't make it a place of sensuality. Matter doesn't mean sin. There was matter long before there was sin, and long after this earth has been purged from all sin by divine fire there will still be matter. God made matter; let's not make matter *sin*.

Why is there food in heaven if we are not expected to satisfy our sense of hunger by eating? Why is rest provided in heaven if there will never be a sense of weariness? Why are there trees, rivers, parks, animals, seas, streets, and rainbows in heaven if we are supposed to become all spirit and be absorbed into God? No, we will not lose our identity by some spiritual osmosis, but we will be people—a redeemed people—enjoying a prepared place that has been tailored to fulfill our Christlike desires. Heaven is as real as its inhabitants.

WHAT HAPPENS WHEN A PERSON DIES?

I believe that when a believer dies, he is instantly caught up into the presence of God, and it's a joyful process. I have seen, heard, and read about people who have had near-death experiences. Ecclesiastes 12:7 states that, at death, the human spirit leaves the body. Jesus confirms the soul's immediate transfer to the afterlife, whether that is heaven or hell, in the parable of the rich man and the beggar Lazarus:

> There was a certain rich man, which was clothed in purple and fine linen, and fared sumptuously every day: And there was a certain beggar named Lazarus,

which was laid at his gate, full of sores, and desiring to be fed with the crumbs which fell from the rich man's table: moreover the dogs came and licked his sores. And it came to pass, that the beggar died, and was carried by the angels into Abraham's bosom: the rich man also died, and was buried; and in hell he lift up his eyes, being in torments, and seeth Abraham afar off, and Lazarus in his bosom.

—LUKE 16:19–23

There is no state of penance or "soul sleep." (See 2 Corinthians 5:6, 8.) As Jesus hung on the cross between two thieves, He said to one of them, "*Today* you will be with Me in Paradise" (Luke 23:43, NKJV, emphasis added). So there should not be dread or a sense of horror about going from this life to the next. We will be caught up with the Lord Jesus immediately upon exiting our earthly body.

WILL WE NEED TO EAT AND DRINK?

Eating and drinking, trees and fruit have been consistent symbols of divine life's availability to mankind from the Garden of Eden through Ezekiel's millennial vision and in the heavenly Jerusalem. These are not three identical pictures; they are progressive steps of a divine revelation. In the Garden of Eden the tree of life sustained the natural life of Adam and Eve. In Ezekiel's millennial vision the trees sustained the earthly inhabitants who would eat of them, but in the New Jerusalem the fruit of the tree of life sustains the life of the resurrected, glorified saints, who form the bride of Christ. It is a higher form of life and requires a superior life-support food, and heaven's tree offers ultra-superior fruit.

John says that each month the trees bear a different crop

of fruit (Revelation 22:2). January may offer pomegranates; February, prunes. March may feature pears, while April may offer peaches. Or the fruit may be something totally unlike anything ever seen on Earth. But it will be appealing, appetizing, life-giving, and varied.

In commenting on this variety of fruit, A. S. Worrell says, "Twelve fruits; that is, twelve harvests each year; representing the constant and abundant blessings that are provided for those who enter that blissful abode."[1]

It may not be necessary to think that every tree will produce the same harvest each month. God may very well stagger the rotation, making each form of fruit available year-round by merely going to a different tree. We have become so accustomed to having Earth's joys become polluted, imperfect, unsatisfying, and short that it is difficult to conceive of heaven's joys being completely pure, perfect, satisfying, and eternal. Though the presence and favor of God in heaven will supply all the wants of His people, meet all their wishes, and fill their hearts with joy, their blessings will never satiate or grow old but will be ever fresh, growing higher and better forever. Fragrant, fresh fruit available in multiple varieties will satisfy the desire to eat, the need for life support, and the fellowship of feasting together.

"But," you may argue, "I can't conceive of saints in their glorified bodies ever hungering or thirsting, or that they would need to eat or drink to replenish energy lost through activity."

Of course, you may be right. We know there will be eating in heaven, but we do not know whether it is done out of necessity or for the pure pleasure of eating. We know from the Old Testament that angels can and do eat, for they ate Sarah's cakes and Abraham's dressed calf (Genesis

18:6–8). We also know that Jesus ate with His disciples after His resurrection (Luke 24:42–43) and that He referred several times to eating and drinking in the kingdom of His glory. Repeatedly He likened the whole provision of grace to a banquet or a feast, and one of the most emphasized scenes of the future is a *supper*, the marriage supper of the Lamb.

There is much that is moral and spiritual in eating. In the sacred rituals of the tabernacle, which was given as a model of heaven, almost everything they did had eating connected with it. Their sacred convocations were called "feasts of the Lord," and all but the whole burnt offering ended up being eaten by the priests or the people. It was through disobedient eating that the Fall and all of its consequences came into the world, so it is to be expected, then, that removal of sin would return man to divinely appointed eating. Seiss reminded us:

> The eating of the fruit of the Tree of Life in the first Paradise was the sacrament of fellowship with life, a commemoration, pledge support, and participation of life eternal, for soul and body. Hence sin cut off man from it; and all the ordinances and ministries of grace since that time are meant for his recovery and readmission to the Tree. Hence also the promise was given to the Church of Ephesus, "To him that overcometh will I give to eat of the Tree of Life, which is in the Paradise of my God" (Revelation 2:7). And so again, "Blessed are they that do his commandments, that they may have right to the tree of life" (Revelation 22:14).[2]

Very much as the golden table of shewbread stood in the holy place of the tabernacle in the wilderness, so the tree of life stands in the way of the golden streets of the New Jerusalem with its monthly fruit for the immortal king-priests of heaven. Eating the special food provided by God for His priests is always scripturally presented as a most precious privilege, and it will be even more so in heaven, for the very eating of these life-fruits speaks of a communion with life, the joy of which exceeds all present comprehension. Our eating may not be so much to sustain life as to sacramentally identify with it. Eating may well be a part of our worship and a means whereby we may fully enjoy God's marvelous provisions for us. As He did to the disciples on the seashore, Christ may often call to us, "Come and dine" (John 21:12). But this time it will not be the coarse food of fishermen—bread and fish—but the palatable food of angels, which was made available in the wilderness as manna and will be obtainable as delicious fruit in heaven, freshly picked from the tree of life.

PERPETUAL HEALING BY DESIGN

Furthermore, these prolific and pleasing trees will provide for the needs of the nations who still reside on the earth. John assures us that "the leaves of the tree were for the healing of the nations" (Revelation 22:2). Fruits for the joys of heaven and leaves for the joys of Earth are the offering of the tree of life. In his commentary on the Book of Revelation, Rev. David Brown, DD, insists, "The *leaves* shall be *health-giving*, not healing, but securing them against sickness."[3] His view is supported by the New Testaments of Weymouth, Moffatt, and Williams, who translate this phrase as "served as medicine for…"; "served to heal…"; "contained the remedy to heal." The emphasis seems to be the giving of strength or preventive medicine rather than a curative remedy, for sin will have been totally removed by this time and the curse will be healed, so we would not expect to find sickness on the earth after the final purging. But since the nations will be peopled with mortals with earthly bodies, some provision must be made to renew their strength, even as God provided for Adam in the garden. But there Adam was allowed to eat of the tree, while here the nations are prohibited entrance to that tree. The city is walled and has guards, and only the heavenly citizens are given access to the tree. But these glorified saints have access to the earth and will serve God as His special agents to the nations on the earth. Whenever we are sent to the earth on a divine mission, we will gather some leaves to take with us. In God's economy there is no waste. There will be no acid smell of burning leaves in heaven. When the leaves start falling, we will merely pick them up and bring them down to the earth to distribute them among the nations, because they will be a source of health and strength to them. This is as close to God's provided tree of life as the nations will get, but it is totally sufficient for their needs, and they will be satisfied. The leaves will be as satisfactory to their form of life as the fruit will be to ours.

SERVICE AS AN ACT OF WORSHIP

As I stated in chapter 1, worship involves more than simply singing hymns. Worshiping God involves our entire being. Our active service to Him is also seen as a form of worship.

Although John saw the authoritarian rule of the divine throne in the New Jerusalem, he did not envision it as a solitary function, for he declared, "And his servants shall serve him: And they shall see his face; and his name shall be in their foreheads" (Revelation 22:3–4). When finally there is no more sin, rebellion, or forgetfulness of the claims of the King, and no more neglect of the word of the eternal Lord, we are going to be able to serve him "in spirit and in truth" (John 4:24). The Greek word John uses here for "serve" is *latreuo*, which is sometimes translated "worship" and other times "serve," so that many of the more recent translations state "shall worship him." It is the word Jesus used in response to Satan's request for worship: "Thou shalt worship the Lord thy God, and him only shalt thou serve [*latreuo*]" (Matthew 4:10). Paul repeatedly used this word in speaking of his service to the Lord. This dual use of the word should create no problems, for the very act of worship involves service. In the Old Testament there is only one Hebrew word used for worship—*shachah*—which is translated ten different ways in the King James Version. Every time it is used it shows activity—something being done as an act of worship. That is why Christians express vocal praise or sing songs as acts of worship—they must do something to worship.

Worship, as we see it in the Book of Revelation, is expressed in adoration, song, praise, and prostration, but it is also expressed in service. We see the mighty angels in adoration and praise, but we also see them actively engaged in the business of their God. They act as God's agents on the earth: they are involved in natural phenomena, they bear God's messages to mankind, and they generally execute God's commands both in heaven and on Earth. Their worship and service intermingle, for their worship expresses their attitude toward God, and their service expresses their obedience to His will.

John suggests that as the angels have served God before the New Jerusalem descends, the saints will serve Him after the city is established. In that day all of the ransomed, all of the redeemed, all of the members of the bride—everyone who is privileged to be a citizen of the New Jerusalem—will be personal servants to the throne. What dignity will be ours! What intimacy with the eternal power and might of the Godhead is accorded to the servants of the most high God! In the Scriptures the prophets and apostles were called "my servants"; during the church age, pastors, priests, evangelists, and missionaries have been called "servants of God"; but in the age to come we will all be classified as His servants. This tells of the nearness to and participation in the administration of divine government that will be granted to us.

But this designation also speaks of mighty activities and responsible duties. Just what these will be is not fully revealed in God's Word, but since they involve the service of God executing the authority of the throne, we can be well assured that they will be tremendous. We will not merely be "doing service"; we will serve by doing the will of God, and that is a mighty will. So much of what we call "serving the Lord" here is halfhearted, self-centered, display-oriented, "make-work" activity, but there all service will be fulfilling the perfect will of God. We will be His servants, His subjects, and life will be in full accord with the divine will.

If you remember, when the queen of Sheba observed the great king Solomon, she was so greatly impressed with the sitting of Solomon's servants, the attendance of his ministers, and their apparel that she exclaimed, "Happy are thy men, happy are these thy servants, which stand continually before thee, and that hear thy wisdom" (1 Kings 10:8). How much happier will we be when we stand before the greater King and hear His wisdom expressed through His council and commands.

The heaven that God revealed to John is not a vast utopia

where the inhabitants sit on fleecy clouds strumming harps of gold and enjoying sensory pleasure; it is a place of intense activity. It is a place of beauty and music; it has magnificent parks and streams of God's pleasure. But it is a kingdom with a King, and the saints have been invited to be involved in God's kingdom as His personal servants.

Joseph A. Seiss comments:

> Such are all the members of the Church of the first-born, the elect, the citizens of the heavenly Jerusalem, the sharers in the administration of that holy kingdom. And of these especially is the word spoken. It tells of the very highest honor and dignity, of the closest intimacy with eternal power and authority, of the most inward nearness and participation in the administration of divine government. But it tells also of mighty activities and responsible duties. It shows us most clearly that the heaven of the glorified saints is not one of idleness. They have something more to do than to sing, and worship, and enjoy. Indeed, the perfection of worship is service, activity for God, the doing of the will of God. And this is to be one of the highest characteristics of the heaven of the saints. They are to do work, heavenly work, the highest kind of work, the execution and administration of the will and bidding of the throne of eternity, the work of the high officials who stand nearest to the throne, and through whom the throne expresses itself. Like "the seven princes of Persia and Media which saw the king's face, and which sat first in the kingdom" (Esther 1:14), so these "servants shall serve him, and they shall see his face, and the name of him shall be upon their forehead."[4]

Not only will it be known that we serve the Lamb of the throne while we stand in the heavens, but whenever we are in active service we will wear God's name on our foreheads, very much as Israel's high priest wore the plate of burnished gold on his forehead, on which was engraved the awesome name of Jehovah. In earlier days the knights emblazed symbols on their crests to show how close to the king they were in his service. Even the men who serve in our armed forces are given symbols and badges that tell us how closely they are related to the commander in chief. However, in heaven the badge of authority will neither be on our shields nor on our uniforms; it will be on our foreheads. All who hear us will know that we do not speak of ourselves but as messengers of the God of heaven.

Furthermore, John declares that "they shall reign for ever and ever" (Revelation 22:5), or for "timeless ages," as Phillips puts it. This is no short-term service; it is endless. It is not a reference back to the service of the millennial period, for that preceded the descent of the New Jerusalem. It is looking forward to the endless eons of eternity when God's original plan will be reestablished for men on the earth. It is a new earth with new people living on it. But whereas in Adam's day the angels ministered as God's agents on the earth, in the new earth the ministers will be the servants of the Lamb from the New Jerusalem. Just as there will be perpetuity of life on the earth, there will be a need for endless government, and Christ will rule the world through His bride. The saints of God will be kings forever and forever, and "the earth shall be filled with the knowledge of the glory of the LORD, as the waters cover the sea" (Habakkuk 2:14; Isaiah 11:9). The dispensing of that knowledge and the revealing of that glory will be the special task of those who bear God's name on their foreheads and who are allowed to see His face.

What living service will be our privilege throughout the coming ages! It will be a living service because it is a dispensing of the very life of God. It will be a loving service because everything will be done as an act of love. And it will be a companionship service—first of all, because we are companions with the throne, and second, because we will be serving side by side with loved ones from whom sickness and death once separated us, but with whom divine life reunited us.

CHAPTER 11

Will I Recognize Loved Ones?

T HE TRANSITORY NATURE of life since the fall of man imposes a continuing series of separations between friends and loved ones. One of the heartaches of old age is the progressive narrowing of the circle of friendships, for each funeral means one less acquaintance on Earth. As a pastor I have been called upon to comfort and strengthen Christians through the shock of death, the pain of burial, and the agony of readjustment. But I have also observed that the long period of loneliness that follows death is far more difficult to overcome than the reality of death itself, for the finality of the loss is overwhelming and without recourse. Nothing but memory lingers, and the longings it produces often bring more pain than pleasure. Here the curse of death constantly haunts the living, but in heaven the curse will be eradicated forever.

WILL CHILDREN WHO NEVER MET THEIR PARENTS RECOGNIZE THEM?

Listening to a Christian telecast, I was pleased to hear the guest tell of her visit to heaven some years ago. She said that although her mother had died in giving her birth, she instantly recognized her, and the mother recognized the full-grown daughter. Some years later a relative showed her a newly discovered tintype group picture, and she quickly picked her mother out from among the group of people, although no other photo of her mother existed. She recognized her mother because she had seen her in heaven.

Of those who have written of their visions or short-term experiences of visiting in heaven, all have expressed an intuitive knowing of those in heaven. Many have testified that the first person they met after entering heaven was a very close loved one. Others have declared that a father or husband conducted them through the river of life. Surely death could not blot out recognition of loved ones, no matter how changed the glorified body may be, for we know one another by tone of voice, style of walk, habit patterns, and ways of expression as much as by physical features.

As a high school student I worked with a blind piano repairman, but our paths separated when I went to college. Many years later, unknown to him, I was visiting in his area and walked up behind him on a dense lawn. Although he was busy talking to a group of people, none of whom knew me, he whirled around and nearly shouted, "Judson! How good to see you again after so many years."

"Chappie," I said, "how could you possibly know it was me?"

"I've spent enough time with you to know you anywhere," he replied.

I doubt if he understood how he recognized people, but in the years that I knew him he was never wrong. Had he developed an inner knowing that escapes those of us who depend upon sight?

By whatever means necessary we will know one another in heaven, and that recognition will trigger reunion. Mothers and fathers will enjoy the thrill of having their children gathered together for a family picnic in heaven's beautiful paradise park. Lovers separated by death will find solace, comfort, and pleasure in each other's arms. Children who died before maturity on Earth can proudly display their development to their mothers and fathers, while the parents rejoice that the death of the earthly body had not impeded the development of the soul and spirit of their children.

Everything that sin has snatched from us, heaven will restore to us—including our Christian loved ones. What a glorious reunion that will be!

There will be so much to discuss and share and so many loved ones to look up that there might be a sense of panic if there were not such an awareness of eternity in everyone.

WHAT WILL WE KNOW, AND WHAT WILL WE REMEMBER?

As I outlined in chapter 1, one of the misconceptions about heaven is that we will know everything once we enter heaven. I believe there will be some things that God will reveal to us when we get to heaven:

> The secret things belong unto the LORD our God: but those things which are revealed belong unto us and to our children for ever.
>
> —DEUTERONOMY 29:29

The phrase "secret things" in the Hebrew is *cathar*, which signifies "to hide by covering; conceal."[1]

In the story of the rich man and Lazarus, Jesus teaches us that our memory goes with us into eternity. On Earth, sin has been a harsh taskmaster that has exacted far more from us than it ever contributed to us. Its pain has greatly exceeded its pleasure. Since experience, though a hard teacher, is a thorough teacher, it is inconceivable that our memories in eternity would ever let us be involved in anything that could cost us our freedom from sin's calloused control. We will have no desire for sin.

WILL KNOWING THAT A LOVED ONE DIDN'T MAKE IT TO HEAVEN MAKE ME SAD?

You may ask, "If in heaven I am aware and recognize saved loved ones, what about the loved ones who did not make it into heaven? Won't their absence produce sorrow and regret?"

Apparently it will not, for we are assured that there will be no sorrow there. If God chooses not to remember our sins (Jeremiah 31:34), then we also will be able to choose not to recall anything that would distract from the joy of heaven.

When those who have had brief visionary trips into paradise were asked if they missed certain loved ones who had rejected Christ on Earth, they have stated that they were totally unaware of their absence. It seems that God blots out the memory of those who chose not to go to heaven and accentuates the awareness of those who have entered in.

My former pastor, Reverend Fuchsia Pickett, illustrated this beautifully in saying that if we are seated in a well-lighted room, it is not possible for us to see out the window into the darkness, but anyone standing in that darkness can see into the room easily. When heaven's Shekinah illuminates all of heaven, there can be no looking out into the darkness into which the lost have been cast eternally. Perhaps they can see us (as was the case in the story Jesus told of the rich man and Lazarus), but if so, it will only increase their torment.

Our ecstasy will not be eclipsed by any sense of tragedy.

God's justice in refusing admittance for the nonrepentant will satisfy every heart, for God's law, not our earthly love, will be the prevailing attitude in heaven.

I do not mean to project that earthly ties will continue into heaven, for marriage is only "until death do us part," but the one factor of eternity that we have been allowed to enter into while still on Earth is love. Love is not earthly but divine: "God is love" (1 John 4:8), and, unlike earthly lust that will pass away with our bodies, it will abide eternally. Whatever measure of true love we have shared with others will carry into eternity, because love is an expression of the soul, not the body. Furthermore, that love will mature and develop to a high degree of perfection when fleshly lusts, earthly fears, and cultural repressions are no longer hindering forces. The divine love we will share with one another in heaven will be imparted by God and shared one with another in an unashamed, unrestricted, and unlimited manner. For many of us who have had great difficulty in expressing tender feelings down here, this release would almost "be heaven" without any of the other benefits.

WILL I RECOGNIZE GREAT CHRISTIAN LEADERS WHOM I HAVE NEVER MET?

Not only will there be joyful reunions with loved ones, but there will also be delightful recognition of and fellowship with members of the bride of Christ who lived in a different span of time or geographical location than we did.

I once spoke from Isaiah to a large gathering of believers in Cincinnati, Ohio. After the service had ended, a sweet sister approached me to say, "Isaiah is my favorite book in the Bible. When I get to heaven I'm going to have a long talk with Isaiah."

"Do you think you will recognize him?" I asked.

"Yes," she said. "I've read his writings so often I believe I'll recognize him from the way he talks."

She is probably right, for in listening to a reading of the Bible it is easy to tell the difference between Peter and Paul, or Moses and Malachi.

How exciting it will be to ask Adam about the first paradise or to discuss the great flood with Noah. What pleasure will be ours as we listen to David sing his psalms to their original tunes or discuss the Song of Solomon with the author. If merely meeting an earthly author produces excitement down here, try to imagine the stimulation of talking with one of the inspired writers of Scripture.

But that will not exhaust our source of fellowship, for the saints of all ages will be there. We will meet Martin Luther, Charles Wesley, John Knox, Charles Spurgeon, and hundreds of others whose lives became milestones on the pathway to heaven. We will listen to the singing of great vocalists who have stirred thousands to holiness and identify with the prayers of men and women who have moved entire communities to God from their prayer closets. We will have a chance to hear some of the great preachers of generations ago and to see how the great variances in theology have merged into one complete picture after men have fully seen that which on Earth could only be partially seen.

We will have the opportunity to thank John Bunyan for writing *The Pilgrim's Progress* while incarcerated and to thank the martyrs who victoriously died, often most painfully and ignominiously, rather than recant their faith. We will meet the pioneers and missionaries who endured such hardships to spread the gospel beyond the borders of Europe and who have made our Christian heritage possible.

To write a complete list of the persons we might want to look up after we arrive in heaven would take another book, but we anticipate meeting these great saints who have so affected our spiritual lives down here on Earth.

WE WILL SEE HIM FACE-TO-FACE.

Yet personally, neither my father, nor my eldest brother, nor the great saints of the ages hold top priority in my desire for fellowship in the New Jerusalem. I long to see Jesus! It is He who took our place, died the death that we deserved, delivered us from sin, purchased our redemption, and brought us into His own residence. Although we have not seen Him, we love Him. He has become the theme of our song, the expression of our confession, the joy of our life, the basis of our blessings, and the foundation of our hope of heaven.

But in spite of all of this we have not really seen Him or known Him. We are acquainted with Him as our need-meeter, but we do not know Him very well as a person. We have learned much about His works and something about His ways, but few have known Him. We have embraced Him as our Savior, received Him as our guide, proclaimed Him as our Lord, but we do not yet know Him as our lover. Paul admitted, "For now we see through a glass, darkly [literally 'as in a riddle']; but then face to face: now I know in part; but then shall I know even as also I am known" (1 Corinthians 13:12). Since most of our earthly knowledge comes to us through our senses, our capacity to receive spiritual knowledge is necessarily limited—we see in a mirror whose silver has darkened with age. But John declares that in heaven "his servants...shall see his face" (Revelation 22:3–4) and that "we shall see him as he is" (1 John 3:2).

Heaven would be glorious even without this, but after

seeing Him as He really is—not as we have imagined Him to be—heaven's joys will be absolutely overwhelming. Moses is the only man in the Bible who was afforded the privilege of face-to-face communication with God, but in heaven it will be available to all of us. If just knowing Him through the letters He wrote (the Bible) has made Christ so precious, try to picture what it will do to us when we actually behold Him intimately.

And we shall see Him "face to face." This is the basis for our hope and the blessing of that hope—interpersonal relationship with Christ Jesus our Lord. This will complete the circle of time, placing it into the circuit of eternity. The era of God and man walking and talking together in paradise's garden, which was lost through Adam's fall, will be restored again, and God's original purpose of creation will be realized—fellowship between creature and Creator with complete understanding, compassionate caring, and companionate sharing.

We are here for a short season as preparation for the hereafter, and now we only sing about seeing Him face-to-face, but in heaven we will experience it, and much more. Personally, I believe that heaven is just this life with all sin removed from it. I am comfortable knowing that heaven is where Jesus abides. Heaven is God's home, His abode, and He will share it with me. That will be the joy of heaven.

Prayer—the Link Between Time and Eternity

I F THE SCRIPTURES were being written in our genera-tion, I suspect that one of the writers would liken prayer to the communication link between spaceship Earth and home-base heaven. Our origins are in God, and He is our final destination, but for our brief sojourn in this time-space dimension of existence, we are physically separated from God.

Prayer is the communication bridge that links heaven and Earth and allows time to pierce into eternity. It permits mortal persons to fellowship and commune with the immortal God, and it provides Him with a channel through which He can communicate with persons far removed from His heaven.

Through the prayer-link communication, we can main-tain a closeness to God's love, wisdom, directions, and interventions into our affairs. When astronauts experience a malfunction of equipment in space, the ground control crew radios a solution to them. Similarly, God makes Himself and His solutions available to us on spaceship Earth.

Until Jesus Christ returns and transforms our earthly bodies into spiritual ones, we are earthlings confined to time—or at least two-thirds of our being is time warped. There is, however, that eternal spirit within us that belongs to eternity. Just as our bodies are uncomfortable in spiritual situations, so our spirits are out of their natural element in this period of time. There is a longing, a groaning, a sighing, even a crying for release from the captivity of earthly bodies. That cry will someday be fulfilled, but for the present, we can release our spirits into the atmosphere of eternity for brief periods by giving ourselves to prayer.

Paul must certainly have experienced this, for he wrote, "We also who have the firstfruits of the Spirit, even we ourselves groan within ourselves, eagerly waiting for the adoption, the redemption of our body" (Romans 8:23, NKJV). But while we wait, we need not continuously imprison our spirits. We can release them into the environment of eternity through prayer.

Three times in two connecting psalms, the psalmist cries, "Why art thou cast down, O my soul? And why art thou disquieted within me? Hope thou in God; for I shall yet praise him for the help of his countenance and my God" (Psalm 42:5). Verse 11 concludes by saying "for I shall yet praise him, who is the health of my countenance, and my God." How often have I feared that I was at the onset of depression when it was nothing more than my spirit complaining about its confinement. When I gave myself to prayer, my spirit began to rejoice, and my whole being came alive. It was not depression. It was oppression of my spirit. My spirit wanted out of its confines for a season of deep breathing of the atmosphere of God in prayer.

SCRIPTURAL PRAYER OUTLASTS TIME.

My personal craving for immortality has driven me to a variety of accomplishments. I have personally supervised the construction of church edifices that will outlast me by many years. I have written books that will probably survive my passing. I rejoice in my three daughters, my grandchildren, and my great-grandchildren. In them, I shall live on after death. Judson Cornwall will not completely pass away at his funeral. Still, all of these extensions are tied to the same time-space dimension in which I am now a prisoner. They are merely earthly accomplishments. They too will pass away.

The only things I have been involved in during my years on Earth that will go into eternity ahead of me and survive forever are the prayers I have prayed in the Spirit. These prayers have reached deep into immortality and have been presented before the throne of God by the mighty angel who has the responsibility to collect the prayers of the saints and mix those prayers with the prayers of Jesus.

When I enter eternity, I will smell the fragrant aroma of heaven. It is beyond description. I know, for I have already smelled it several times. When I wrote my first book, *Let Us Praise*, the room frequently filled with the divine aroma. After gaining entrance to heaven, I will see the clouds of incense and smell its unique blend of fragrances. Then I will know part of that odor is the prayers I prayed while still traveling on spaceship Earth.

Prayer is the only eternal thing we do while here on Earth. Many of our activities affect our eternal life to come, but prayer participates in it right now. When we incorporate the Scriptures into our praying, we not only enter the eternity of our future, but we also get involved in the eternity of our past and present, for God's Word is, was, and shall always be. We do not fully comprehend God's eternal now, but when we pray His Word, we become involved in it right here on the earth.

NOTES

PREFACE
ABOUT THIS BOOK

1. Cathy Lynn Grossman, "View of God Can Reveal Your Values and Politics," *USA Today*, September 12, 2006, A1.
2. Ibid.
3. Ibid.
4. Judson Cornwall, interview with Stephen Strang, n.d., on his last book, *Dying With Grace*.
5. Ibid.
6. Basilea Schlink, *What Comes After Death?* (Carol Stream, IL: Creation House, 1976), 119.

CHAPTER 1
IS HEAVEN A REAL PLACE?

1. Judson Cornwall, *Let Us Draw Near* (Plainfield, NJ: Logos, 1977), preface.

CHAPTER 2
WHAT IS HEAVEN LIKE?

1. Smith Wigglesworth, *Smith Wigglesworth on Heaven: God's Great Plan for Your Life* (New Kensington, PA: Whitaker House, 1998), 74.

CHAPTER 3
HOW DIFFERENT WILL OUR HEAVENLY HOME BE FROM OUR EARTHLY HOME?

1. Schlink, *What Comes After Death?* 73.

2. John Albert Bengel, *New Testament Word Studies*, vol. 1 (Grand Rapids, MI: Kregel Publications, 1978), 682.

3. M. R. Vincent, *Word Studies in the New Testament* (MacDill AFB, FL: MacDonald Publishing Co., reprint of 1888 edition), 484.

4. Robert Jamieson, A.R. Fausset, and David Brown, *A Commentary: Critical, Experimental and Practical on the Old and New Testaments*, vol. 5 (Grand Rapids, MI: Wm. B. Eerdmans, 1948), 433.

5. Matthew Henry, *Commentary on the Whole Bible* (Grand Rapids, MI: Zondervan Publishing House, 1961), 1589.

CHAPTER 4
WHERE IS IT, AND HOW DO WE GET THERE?

1. The Old Testament books of the Bible that do not mention heaven are Numbers, Ruth, Esther, Song of Solomon, Obadiah, and Micah. The New Testament books of the Bible that do not mention heaven are 1 and 2 Timothy, Titus, Philemon, 2 and 3 John, and Jude, the last three of which are single-chapter books.

2. Robert Baker Girdlestone, *Synonyms of the Old Testament* (Grand Rapids, MI: Wm. B. Eerdmans Publishing Co., reprint of second edition of 1897), 267.

3. Edward M. Bounds, *Heaven: A Place, a City, a Home* (Grand Rapids, MI: Baker Book House, paperback edition, 1975), 20–21.

4. Biblesoft, *Biblesoft's New Exhaustive Strong's Numbers and Concordance with Expanded Greek-Hebrew Dictionary*, PC Study Bible v3, copyright © 1994, Biblesoft and International Bible Translators, Inc., s.v. *parerchomai*, NT:3928.

5. William R. Newell, *Book of the Revelation* (Chicago, IL: Grace Publications, 1935), 352.

6. Judson Cornwall, *Dying With Grace* (Lake Mary, FL: Charisma House, 2004), 123.

7. Ibid., 119–120, 124. If you have received Jesus Christ into your heart or would like prayer or more information about your relationship with God, please contact us at pray4me@strang.com.

CHAPTER 5
THE NEW JERUSALEM: FACT OR FICTION?

1. Newell, *Book of the Revelation*, 352.

2. As of 2006, the world population had reached 6.5 billion people. (David Leonard, "World Population Hits 6.5 Billion," February 25, 2006, MSNBC.com, http://www.msnbc.msn.com/id/11545564/ [accessed January 22, 2007].) According to the United Nations Population Division, the world population is expected to increase to 9 billion by 2050. (United Nations Population Division, Department of Economic and Social Affairs, *World Population Prospects: The 2004 Revision Population Database*, http://esa.un.org/unpp/index.asp?panel=4 [accessed January 22, 2007].)

CHAPTER 6
WHAT WILL THE NEW JERUSALEM BE LIKE?

1. A. C. Gaebelein, *The Annotated Bible: The Holy Scriptures Analyzed and Annotated*, vol. 9 (Wheaton, IL: Van Kampen Press, 1913), 278.

2. Adam Clarke, *The New Testament of Our Lord and Saviour Jesus Christ*, vol. 6 (New York: Abingdon-Cokesbury Press, n.d.), 1061.

3. A. S. Worrell, *New Testament of Our Lord and Saviour Jesus Christ, a Translation* (Springfield, MO: Gospel Publishing House, n.d.), 394.

4. Gaebelein, *The Annotated Bible*, 278.

5. J. A. Seiss, *The Apocalypse*, vol. 3 (Philadelphia: Philadelphia School of the Bible, 1865), 425.

6. Loren Fox, *One Hour Inside the Pearly Gates* (Springfield, MO: Gospel Publishing House, n.d.), 9.

7. Seiss, *The Apocalypse*, 427.

CHAPTER 7
HOW DIFFERENT WILL THE NEW EARTH BE FROM THE OLD EARTH?

1. Cornwall, *Let Us Draw Near*.

2. Vincent, *Word Studies in the New Testament*, 643.

3. Wikipedia.com, "Crusades," http://en.wikipedia.org/wiki/The_crusades#_note-0 (accessed January 24, 2007).

4. Robert Tuck, *The Preacher's Complete Homiletic Commentary on the New Testament*, vol. 11 (New York: Funk & Wagnalls Co., n.d), 569.

5. Bounds, *Heaven: A Place, a City, a Home*, 86–87.

CHAPTER 8
WHAT WILL LIFE IN HEAVEN BE LIKE?

1. Bounds, *Heaven: A Place, a City, a Home*, 69.

2. Seiss, *The Apocalypse*, 433.

CHAPTER 10
WHAT WILL MY BODY LOOK LIKE?

1. Worrell, *New Testament of Our Lord and Saviour Jesus Christ, a Translation*, 395.

2. Seiss, *The Apocalypse*, 430–431.

3. Jamieson, Fausset, and Brown, *A Commentary: Critical, Experimental and Practical on the Old and New Testaments*, 722.

4. Seiss, *The Apocalypse*, vol. 3, 440–441.

CHAPTER 11
WILL I RECOGNIZE LOVED ONES?

1. Biblesoft, *Biblesoft's New Exhaustive Strong's Numbers and Concordance with Expanded Greek-Hebrew Dictionary*, s.v. *cathar*, OT:5641.

SCRIPTURE INDEX

Genesis

Genesis 1:28   *6, 54*
Genesis 2   *28*
Genesis 2:5, 8   *23*
Genesis 2:9   *85*
Genesis 2:10   *79*
Genesis 2:15   *16*
Genesis 2:17   *85*
Genesis 3   *28*
Genesis 3:16–19   *122*
Genesis 5:3, 5   *20*
Genesis 18:6–8   *138*
Genesis 24:53   *117*
Genesis 28:17   *9*

Exodus

Exodus 19:6   *90*
Exodus 28:15–21   *59*
Exodus 28:17–21   *75*
Exodus 30:20   *99*

Leviticus

Leviticus 26:12   *114*

Numbers

Numbers 10:33   *39*
Numbers 21:17   *82*

Deuteronomy

Deuteronomy 6:10–11   *39*
Deuteronomy 10:14   *46*
Deuteronomy 29:29   *149*

2 Samuel

2 Samuel 22:7   *9*

1 Kings

1 Kings 8:27   *9, 45*
1 Kings 10:8   *143*

Nehemiah

Nehemiah 2:8   *18*

Esther

Esther 1:14   *144*

Psalms

Psalm 8:3–4   *viii*
Psalm 9:4   *126*
Psalm 15:1–2   *115*
Psalm 19:1   *111*
Psalm 19:1–2   *44*
Psalm 22:3   *114*
Psalm 24:1–2   *129*
Psalm 33:6   *44*
Psalm 36:8–9   *81*
Psalm 37:9, 11, 29   *53*
Psalm 42:5   *156*
Psalm 42:11   *156*
Psalm 46:4   *80*
Psalm 47   *128*
Psalm 47:1–9   *129*
Psalm 68:18   *23*
Psalm 84:11   *34*
Psalm 86:9   *129*

Psalm 90:17   *116*
Psalm 100:4   *77*
Psalm 100:5   *121*
Psalm 102:19   *9*
Psalm 115:16   *46*
Psalm 128:3   *6*
Psalm 137:5–6   *52*
Psalm 149:4   *56, 112, 116*

Proverbs

Proverbs 2   *6*
Proverbs 3   *6*
Proverbs 8:31   *56*
Proverbs 18:15   *6*
Proverbs 25:4   *120*

Ecclesiastes

Ecclesiastes 2:5   *18*
Ecclesiastes 12:7   *21, 136*

Song of Solomon

Song of Solomon 4:13   *18*
Song of Solomon 5:16   *70*

Isaiah

Isaiah 6:1   *9*
Isaiah 11:9   *145*
Isaiah 25:6   *5*
Isaiah 26:1   *74*
Isaiah 44:6   *46*
Isaiah 45:18   *65*
Isaiah 51:11   *5*
Isaiah 55:9   *63*
Isaiah 57:15   *45*

Isaiah 60:13   *73*
Isaiah 60:18   *74, 77*
Isaiah 60:21   *53*
Isaiah 61:1, 3   *116*
Isaiah 62:6   *77*
Isaiah 63:15   *45*
Isaiah 65:21   *5*
Isaiah 65:25   *5*
Isaiah 66:1   *10, 55*
Isaiah 66:22–23   *5*

Jeremiah

Jeremiah 31:34   *150*

Ezekiel

Ezekiel 8:6   *55*
Ezekiel 47:1–12   *79*
Ezekiel 47:7, 12   *5*

Daniel

Daniel 2:22   *16*
Daniel 12:2   *22*

Hosea

Hosea 14:6   *116*

Habakkuk

Habakkuk 2:14   *145*

Zephaniah

Zephaniah 3:17   *6*

Zechariah

Zechariah 14:20–21   *102*

Malachi

Malachi 3:17   *116*

Matthew

Matthew 4:10   *142*
Matthew 5:5   *53*
Matthew 5:34   *10*
Matthew 6:10   *123*
Matthew 6:33   *xiii, 130*
Matthew 13:45–46   *77*
Matthew 22:29–30   *6*
Matthew 23:38   *33*
Matthew 24:15   *100*
Matthew 25:31   *103*
Matthew 25:31, 34   *87*
Matthew 26:29   *133*
Matthew 27:52–53   *23*
Matthew 28:18   *130*

Mark

Mark 13:31   *53*

Luke

Luke 11:9   *131*
Luke 11:20   *131*
Luke 12:32   *34*
Luke 14:15   *5*
Luke 15:25   *33*
Luke 16:15   *100*
Luke 16:19–23   *137*
Luke 16:19–31   *19*
Luke 16:22   *21*
Luke 17:21   *131*
Luke 22:30   *5*

Luke 23   *28*
Luke 23:43   *19, 137*
Luke 24   *7*
Luke 24:42–43   *139*

John

John 1:4   *94, 109*
John 1:14   *8*
John 2:10   *133*
John 2:16   *33*
John 3:3   *132*
John 3:8   *113*
John 4:14   *109*
John 4:24   *142*
John 5:26   *109*
John 6:33   *110*
John 6:48   *109*
John 6:53–54   *86, 109*
John 6:63, 69   *110*
John 7:37–39   *112*
John 7:38   *82*
John 8:12   *96*
John 8:44   *3*
John 10:10   *110*
John 11:25   *110*
John 13:36   *32*
John 14:1   *36*
John 14:2   *9, 36*
John 14:3   *40, 41, 47, 49, 55*
John 14:6–7   *58*
John 14:23   *36*
John 14:30   *120*
John 15:11   *17, 107*
John 16:8   *130*
John 16:13   *113*

John 16:14   *130*
John 17:24   *35*
John 20:17   *32*
John 21:12   *140*

Acts

Acts 1:9–11   *48*
Acts 2:2   *113*
Acts 7:55   *10*
Acts 17:28   *94, 122*
Acts 26:18   *95*

Romans

Romans 3:23   *58, 104*
Romans 4:13   *53*
Romans 5:8   *58*
Romans 6:23   *58*
Romans 8:9, 11   *114*
Romans 8:9–23   *121*
Romans 8:23   *156*
Romans 8:38–39   *32*
Romans 14:17   *131*

1 Corinthians

1 Corinthians 2:9   *15, 87*
1 Corinthians 2:9–10   *57, 133*
1 Corinthians 10:21   *86*
1 Corinthians 11:20   *86*
1 Corinthians 12:4–11   *113*
1 Corinthians 13:12   *16, 92, 153*
1 Corinthians 15:44   *135*
1 Corinthians 15:45, 47   *135*

1 Corinthians 15:49   *135*
1 Corinthians 15:52–54   *7*
1 Corinthians 15:54   *107*

2 Corinthians

2 Corinthians 2:11   *3*
2 Corinthians 5:1–5   *27*
2 Corinthians 5:6, 8   *24, 137*
2 Corinthians 5:8   *22*
2 Corinthians 5:17   *53, 58*
2 Corinthians 5:20   *104*
2 Corinthians 6:16   *114*
2 Corinthians 12   *28*
2 Corinthians 12:2   *19, 45*
2 Corinthians 12:4   *19, 27*

Galatians

Galatians 4:26   *62*
Galatians 5:22–23   *86, 113*

Ephesians

Ephesians 1:12   *56*
Ephesians 1:14   *105, 129*
Ephesians 1:20–23   *49*
Ephesians 1:22–23   *94*
Ephesians 2:8–9   *58*
Ephesians 2:19   *104*
Ephesians 2:20–21   *75*
Ephesians 3:17   *114*
Ephesians 3:21   *54*
Ephesians 4:8   *23*
Ephesians 4:11–12   *130*
Ephesians 5:27   *56, 116*

Philippians

Philippians 1:6   *112*
Philippians 3:20   *104*
Philippians 4:8   *69*

Colossians

Colossians 1:16   *56*
Colossians 1:27   *10*
Colossians 3:1   *xiii*
Colossians 4:2–3   *97*

1 Thessalonians

1 Thessalonians 4:14,
   16–18   *41*
1 Thessalonians 4:16   *24*
1 Thessalonians 4:16–17   *22*
1 Thessalonians 5:21   *102*

1 Timothy

1 Timothy 3:16   *10*

Hebrews

Hebrews 1:14   *22*
Hebrews 3:1   *103*
Hebrews 4:16   *10, 126*
Hebrews 8:2   *7, 9*
Hebrews 8:5   *8*
Hebrews 11:8–10   *48*
Hebrews 11:10   *46, 62, 70*
Hebrews 11:13   *46, 104*
Hebrews 11:16   *47*
Hebrews 11:36–38   *105*
Hebrews 12:2   *112*
Hebrews 12:22   *11, 47, 70*

Hebrews 12:22–23   *17, 91*
Hebrews 12:23   *24*
Hebrews 13:14   *47*

1 Peter

1 Peter 1:6–9   *18*
1 Peter 1:7   *117*
1 Peter 1:19   *117*
1 Peter 2:6   *117*
1 Peter 2:7   *117*
1 Peter 3:18   *56*
1 Peter 4:12–13   *28*

2 Peter

2 Peter 1:1   *117*
2 Peter 1:4   *12, 117*
2 Peter 3:6   *53*
2 Peter 3:10   *52*

1 John

1 John 1:5   *93*
1 John 1:9   *58*
1 John 3:2   *xvi, 103, 113, 153*
1 John 4:1   *101*
1 John 4:8   *151*

Revelation

Revelation 1:6   *96*
Revelation 2   *28, 110, 139*
Revelation 2:7   *5, 19, 25,*
   110, 139
Revelation 2:10   *110*
Revelation 3:5   *110*
Revelation 3:8   *97*

Revelation 3:21 25
Revelation 4:2–3 72
Revelation 4:3 74
Revelation 4:11 56
Revelation 5:10 96
Revelation 6:10 6
Revelation 7:9–10 67
Revelation 7:10 74
Revelation 7:15 16
Revelation 11:11 110
Revelation 11:15 54
Revelation 12:10 74
Revelation 13:6 3
Revelation 14:2–3 5
Revelation 15:2 99
Revelation 17:4–5 100
Revelation 17:14 129
Revelation 19:9 133
Revelation 19:16 96
Revelation 20:12 104
Revelation 20:12–14 xvi
Revelation 21 56, 61, 71,
    100, 110
Revelation 21:1 62
Revelation 21:2 61, 103
Revelation 21:3 55, 57, 115
Revelation 21:4 17, 106
Revelation 21:5 122
Revelation 21:6 110
Revelation 21:8 102
Revelation 21:9 61
Revelation 21:10–14 71
Revelation 21:11 71, 74
Revelation 21:12 73, 77
Revelation 21:14 75

Revelation 21:16 63, 65
Revelation 21:17 73
Revelation 21:18, 21 75
Revelation 21:21 77, 78
Revelation 21:22 90
Revelation 21:23 93
Revelation 21:24 62, 95
Revelation 21:25 77, 97, 98
Revelation 21:27 99, 100,
    101, 104
Revelation 22 28, 71, 110
Revelation 22:1 79, 81, 110
Revelation 22:2 5, 84, 138,
    140
Revelation 22:2, 14 110
Revelation 22:3 118, 126
Revelation 22:3–4 141, 153
Revelation 22:5 98, 145
Revelation 22:12 133
Revelation 22:14 134, 139
Revelation 22:17 110
Revelation 22:20 134

THE MOMENT *life* OF STEPPING FROM THIS INTO THE NEXT SHOULD NOT BE ONE WE DREAD OR FEAR!

If you have been encouraged and challenged by
Things You Don't Know About Heaven, here are two more
books by Judson Cornwall you will enjoy:

Embark for Heaven Without Fear
Cornwall offers a guided step-by-step
process that will help you remove the
fear often attached to dying and replace
it with a response of joy. Discover how
God can give you grace to take each
step from this life to eternal life.

978-1-59185-453-1 / $10.99

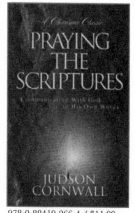

978-0-88419-266-4 / $11.99

Amplify Your Prayer Life
One of the most frustrating aspects of
prayer is not being able to find the right
words to express what dwells deep within
your heart. Learn how to bring the
Scriptures into your personal prayer life for
a closer relationship with the Father.

Visit your local bookstore!